The ALICE *Behind*

WONDERLAND

ALSO BY SIMON WINCHESTER

The ALICE Behind

WONDERLAND

SIMON
WINCHESTER

OXFORD
UNIVERSITY PRESS

OXFORD
UNIVERSITY PRESS

Oxford University Press, Inc., publishes works that further
Oxford University's objective of excellence
in research, scholarship, and education.

Oxford   New York
Auckland   Cape Town   Dar es Salaam   Hong Kong   Karachi
Kuala Lumpur   Madrid   Melbourne   Mexico City   Nairobi
New Delhi   Shanghai   Taipei   Toronto

With offices in
Argentina   Austria   Brazil   Chile   Czech Republic   France   Greece
Guatemala   Hungary   Italy   Japan   Poland   Portugal   Singapore
South Korea   Switzerland   Thailand   Turkey   Ukraine   Vietnam

Published by Oxford University Press, Inc.
198 Madison Avenue, New York, NY 10016

www.oup.com

Oxford is a registered trademark of Oxford University Press

Library of Congress Cataloging-in-Publication Data
Winchester, Simon.
The Alice behind wonderland / by Simon Winchester.
p.   cm.
ISBN 978-0-19-539619-5
1. Carroll, Lewis, 1832–1898. Alice's adventures in Wonderland.
2. Carroll, Lewis, 1832–1898.—Photograph collections.
3. Great Britain—Social life and customs—19th century
4. Hargreaves, Alice Pleasance Liddell, 1852–1934.
5. Fantasy fiction, English—History and criticism.
6. Children's stories, English—History and criticism.
7. Alice (Fictitious character : Carroll). I. Title.
PR4611.A73W56   2011
823'.8—dc22   2010053503

Photograph of Alice Liddell courtesy of Morris L. Parrish Collection,
Department of Rare Books and Special Collections, Princeton University Library

1 3 5 7 9 8 6 4 2

Printed in the United States of America
on acid-free paper

FOR CYBELE

CONTENTS

The ALICE *Behind*

WONDERLAND

Chapter One

THE PHOTOGRAPH IN QUESTION

ON THE MAIN FLOOR OF THE FIRESTONE LIBRARY, THE COZILY
magnificent and prematurely ancient (it was built in 1948) Gothic
centerpiece of the Princeton University campus, there is what
appears to be the private library of an English gentleman's country
house, carefully set back and hidden away to keep it from the general bustle of readers.

Beyond its collection of leather-bound books, this room-with-
in-a-room is notable for its deep and corduroy-ribbed reading
chairs, stained glass, richly polished paneling, lamps, and portraits.
Perhaps most impressive of all to those of romantic disposition is
its baronial fireplace—in which, however, no fire is ever permitted
to be lit because of its being sited within a great and very flamma-
ble academic library.

The room is more than just a faithful reproduction of the
library—it *is* the library, reconstructed panel by panel, carpet by

carpet, book by book—the library of a mansion, Dormy House, built some thirty miles away in the tiny New Jersey hamlet of Pine Valley, a swanky Philadelphia suburb, really. The house was owned by a wealthy financier, Morris Longstreth Parrish, a Princeton alumnus whose passions were many, though few so great as that for collecting Victorian books.

Parrish & Company was a prominent Philadelphia stock-broking firm, a member of the exchange from the end of the nineteenth century, and owned by a colonial-era family long prominent in Main Line society. Well traveled and well rounded, Morris Parrish never graduated from Princeton. His wealth and other interests much distracted him from his studies. But as a young man he developed a keen interest in books. He read everything he could, furiously, though he much preferred the Victorian and Edwardian classics to later twentieth-century novels, which he generally disdained, though he prized them as objects later. Nonetheless, reading was all. He abhorred dust jackets, slip cases, penciled prices marked inside the cover—and unread books. "A collector who has unopened books is to me an enigma," he once wrote. "He cannot, of course, read them; and no-one can deny that if a book cannot be read, it loses its purpose of existence."

He started collecting in the early 1890s, his initial aim the perfection of his parents' collection of Charles Dickens novels, which his father had bought edition by edition as they were published. Morris made an early and ill-advised decision to rebind some of these volumes for his father in glossy red leather, learning betimes that the smartest collectors strived not to prettify their books, but to maintain them in a state as close as possible to their original condition. From then on, a steely determination settled on Parrish, and with little care for expense he set about ensuring that every book he acquired was in near-original condition. Dealers soon recognized what he wanted (and what he could afford): the term "in Parrish condition" is still employed in the antiquarian book trade to denote books of such quality as to represent the apotheosis of the collector's art.

It was during the Great War that Parrish's collecting zeal and acumen came to be widely recognized—and before long, dealers around the world were helping him complete full-spectrum runs of all the authors he admired. From the Brontës to Robert Louis Stevenson, from Sir James Barrie to Charlotte Yonge, he collected everything—every book, every edition, every pamphlet, playbill, poster, binding, variant and foreign-language version ever made—so he could rightly claim to have the world's best and most comprehensive collection of English Victorian fiction.

By the time he died in 1944, Parrish's formal Victorian library amounted to approximately sixty-five hundred volumes, representing the careers-in-full of the authors he most favored—Thackeray, Carlyle, Trollope, Wilkie Collins, Dickens, Bulwer-Lytton, and Froude among them—and most comprehensively, almost the entire oeuvre of the Christ Church, Oxford, mathematics lecturer Charles Lutwidge Dodgson, now more familiarly known as Lewis Carroll. (The first manuscript of *Alice's Adventures in Wonderland* is in London, and a few scores of the good photographs are scattered in libraries around the world; almost everything else is in the Parrish.)

All of these authors' books, and more than a thousand manuscripts—mostly letters by and to them—were then left to Princeton, his alma mater having given him, perhaps in the spirit of fondly appreciated anticipation, an honorary degree in 1939, five years before he died. The collection he bequeathed is now worth untold millions.

Thus it is that either in a vault below or on a bookshelf close to the unusable, chimneyless fireplace there stand, among a host of other valuable and worthy books, a few very large volumes of pictures, each one edged in nut-brown morocco and covered in buckram. On the front of each, embossed in gold leaf and within an ornamented morocco cartouche-shaped adhesion, are stamped the words "Photographic Scrap Book," and below, a volume number. Four such volumes are in the Parrish Room, and they are much revered and fretted over. They were made a century and a half ago in Oxford by Dodgson and contain so much, and tell so very much, about a multiplicity of things.

The four volumes had been created as collections of his photographs in the 1870s, privately, by Dodgson himself; and while they were certainly intended for the safekeeping of the pictures, they were also meant for display. Known in the vernacular of the time as "show albums," their principal purpose was to provide evening entertainment for the polite and sedate drawing-room audiences to whom they would be proudly shown by their shy, half-deaf, and stuttering creator.

Almost any one of the photographs they contain could tell a story—they are works of a distinctly narrative art. But on page 65 of volume 2 there is one picture in particular that has excited public interest over the years. The second of the four volumes at Princeton contains 134 rather stiff and evidently high-quality rag-paper pages, almost all of which have a half-page photograph fastened to them with adhesive. The remaining space is given over to a neatly prepared caption, written with a fountain pen in blue ink by a clear if somewhat childlike hand.

As it happens, the first page of the album is blank; a caption suggests that an image of the Prince of Wales was intended for it.

Only the signature of His Royal Highness now remains below where the image might have been: Arthur A. Edward V, signed at Frewen Hall, Oxford, on December 13, 1860.

Page 2 contains the volume's first photograph, depicting two small girls, each dressed in a ceremonial Chinese silk *qipao*, with a large bamboo umbrella open behind to shelter them from an imaginary sun. There are many photographs of small girls in the pages that follow, though the very next page is blank, like the first, with a caption indicating that the space had been reserved for the portrait of a parsonage in Cheshire.

Following on from this slightly uneven beginning, the album picks up pace, and on page after page captions are matched to photographs. There are only a couple of blanks and items promised but missing.

Close to the middle of the book, and after dozens of somewhat tedious sepia portraits of frocked, solemn, and elderly divines—the long-forgotten reverends Rankin, Salmon, and Keane most notable among them—we come finally to page 65.

Were it not for the hush of the carpeted library room, and the hushed bustle of readers passing through the Firestone corridors beyond—a viewer might cry out, startled. For the picture is of no fustian'd cleric of advancing years, nor of the parsonage in which he might have lodged. It is instead of a young girl, seven years old maybe, naked of shoulder and chest and dressed in decorously disarranged linen rags.

She is lazing coquettishly against a crumbling garden wall of limestone and sandstone, standing in a corner in her bare feet. She looks with a calm directness right into the camera lens, her face bearing an expression quite unutterably different from those in all the previous images. It is an expression of impish, secret knowledge, a winsome look that manages to be both confident and disturbing. Many who view it find it vaguely unsettling to return the young girl's gaze, and not a few move on to other pages, or close the book and return it to the shelves. Yet, for most, even after the book is finally shut and put back, the memory of the image proves hauntingly and lingeringly distracting, and for a long while.

The picture is a formal portrait of Alice Pleasance Liddell, the daughter of the dean of Christ Church College, Oxford, the great classicist and lexicographer Henry Liddell (a punctilious man who pronounced his name with the stress on the last syllable). Charles Dodgson, who had befriended the girl and already photographed her several times, encouraged her on this occasion to dress for him as a starveling and beggar-maid. The result is one of the most memorable photographic likenesses ever taken, freighted not just with uneasy resonances, but having later powerful literary consequences and associations that remain with us to this day.

It is a reasonably sizable picture, a direct contact print (proper enlargement not being an option in those days) from the glass-plate negative on which the image was first captured by Dodgson's camera. It measures 6 5/8 inches high, and 5 1/8 inches wide, filling about half of the album page. The top of the image has been rather decorously arched, or domed, to give it the appearance of a cloister. Other shapes chosen by Dodgson for his album—horizontal and vertical ovals, chamfered rectangles, perfect squares, circles, half-moons—would scarcely have suited the dignity of this college setting. The frame had to be suitable to the site, so it is somewhat formal, even vaguely ecclesiastical.

The background is stone—newish-looking blocks of masonry on the deanery wall to the left of the picture, well-worn and rather flakier old stone in the garden wall behind. Both the house wall and the garden wall are made from the Jurassic coral limestones and sandy limestones found in the quarries outside Oxford—in places such as Chipping Norton—and described in loving detail by W. J. Arkell, the official historian of the Oxonian Mesozoic.

Alice is standing in a batten-bordered corner of the shrubbery, one foot treading indelicately on a small cluster of nasturtiums, her right side brushing against and forcing back a tall cloud of clematis. The condition of the plants the girl disturbs seems noteworthy—many of the leaves are upturned and bruised. This is of some forensic interest: by their appearance they would seem already to have been trampled upon that day—probably during Dodgson's attempt on that same summer's afternoon to take a photograph of Alice dressed in her best finery. In that picture the plants are relatively undisturbed; in this one, some mayhem appears to have been committed by the child's feet. We can conclude, then, that the better-dressed picture was taken first, and that only after it was done was the little girl invited to change and to pose again. Only a small nugget from that day's rich historical mine, perhaps, but maybe just worthy of record.

In the earlier picture—we shall assume the chronology is correct: formal picture first, informal second—she is wearing short white ankle socks and black patent-leather shoes. In the second—the picture that is our subject—her feet are quite naked. However, to protect them from the gravel and sharper stones scattered at the garden's edge someone has placed on the ground a rough-looking carpet, apparently made of sisal, and probably hauled into the garden from the nearby greenhouse. It is set down in front of the wooden batten and across to the place where Dodgson has established his tripod. Alice's right foot is placed on it, and since it is this foot that would have borne her weight for the time required for the exposure of the glass-plate negative, she, a naturally fidgety child, would no doubt have appreciated having it.

The girl stands, leaning very slightly back, though not apparently touching the garden wall, in a seductive pose. Her left arm is crooked and the hand placed on her waist, the fist half-closed. Her right arm is bent in front of her at waist level, her hand cupped in a posture of a person hoping to receive alms, or else a benison of some kind. Her hair is newly washed and gleaming, cut in pageboy style, bobbed and with a fringe, parted in a line directly above her slightly retroussé nose.

The condition of her hair perhaps undermines her playing with complete success the role for which Dodgson has selected her. He had wanted her to portray for his camera a beggar-girl, a slum-child from some pestilential home, a girl compelled by poverty or parental order to induce passersby to drop funds into her upturned palm. But the skeptical would instantly see through this ruse: the girl's hair is just too neat and clean, her face too smooth and fine of feature, and her limbs suspiciously free of blemish or scar. This is a young girl in reverse fancy dress, amused by her brief excursion into the harsh world of the mendicant. This is the daughter of the dean of Christ Church, accustomed to candlelit halls and sanctuaries of calm and incense—not a waif habitually found on London street corners, begging from toffs.

And her cotton or linen shift is no great disguise, either. It is ragged, certainly—and in the image held by the Parrish Collection a tear in the negative makes it appear even more so, as though there were a great circular rent above her (mysteriously invisible) left knee. (The only other extant print, also held by Princeton in the Cotsen Children's Collection, is from Reginald Southey's album and is of slightly better quality when it comes to the left knee.) But the garment has been decorously disarranged—her shoulders both visible, her elbows and lower arms, and her chest and her tiny left nipple. The shift is folded and tucked above her waist so that it falls double, but has been shortened to reveal her calves and, of course, her slender ankles and her surprisingly large feet. There is sufficient shoulder, ankle, and skin revealed about Miss Liddell to excite and, these days, to infuriate; and also, for the passing skeptic, there is such an abundance of the meretricious in the image for him to exclaim, sotto voce, *I don't think so*. This is an act, a tiny player in her costume.

A costume inspired, as it happens, by the premier poet of the day, Alfred, Lord Tennyson. His brief narrative of the fabled meeting between the North African king Cophetua and the beggar-maid Penelophon inspired Victorian artists—Burne-Jones, Rossetti, and Holman Hunt most famously among them; and the stanzas, first published in 1842, had long been inscribed upon every beating heart in the land, young Charles Dodgson's included.

> Her arms across her breast she laid;
> She was more fair than words can say:
> Bare-footed came the beggar maid
> Before the king Cophetua.
> In robe and crown the king stept down,
> To meet and greet her on her way;
> "It is no wonder," said the lords,
> "She is more beautiful than day."
> As shines the moon in clouded skies,
> She in her poor attire was seen:

THE PHOTOGRAPH IN QUESTION

One praised her ankles, one her eyes,
One her dark hair and lovesome mien:
So sweet a face, such angel grace,
In all that land had never been:
Cophetua sware a royal oath:
"This beggar maid shall be my queen!"

And thus, so carefully staged by the ardently artistic Dodgson, does young Alice appear—barefoot, one arm across her middle, ankles in full view, and clad in poor attire—yet with "so sweet a face, such angel grace." It was a degree of grace that would set into motion something of even greater moment in England and the world beyond than the marriage of King Cophetua himself.

Chapter Two

THE PHOTOGRAPHER-TO-BE

CHARLES LUTWIDGE DODGSON WAS A FEW WEEKS INTO HIS TWENTY-FIFTH
year when, on March 18, 1856, he purchased his first mahogany-
and-brass folding camera and began his quarter-century career as
an amateur portrait photographer. At the time, he was a junior fellow at Christ Church College, Oxford; was a sub-librarian, a
scholarship holder, and a college lecturer in mathematics; and had
a suite of top-floor rooms in Tom Quad—through the ancient ceil-
ing of which he would later, and somewhat incredibly, persuade the
old and very traditional college to allow him to punch a skylight to
turn the room into a studio. He further convinced them to let him
use the deanery garden a few paces away as the stage set.

But this was all a very long way from Daresbury, in Cheshire,
where Dodgson had been born on January 27, 1832.

Dodgson's father, also named Charles, was a learned High
Church prelate of decided opinions who was appointed initially to

a position well beneath his intellectual merit—as what was called a "perpetual curate." He was assigned to All Saint's Church in what was then a pleasantly remote North Country village of no more than 150 people. Charles was the third of eleven children born to the parson and to his wife and third cousin, Frances Lutwidge. He also happened to be the first son, a position that would bring in train all the cumbersome responsibilities and duties of care inherent in Victorian primogeniture. Such duties included his being predestined to take care of the Dodgson tribe in the event that his parents ever faltered, and he assumed that responsibility with grave seriousness and a powerful sense of Christian devotion.

The trials of these duties would intrude only in later years. The first eleven years of his life were spent in "complete seclusion from the world," in Daresbury, the little village a few miles inland from Liverpool. The years in Daresbury, "this island-farm—broad seas of corn, stirred by the wandering breath of morn—the happy spot where I was born," turned out to be formative and happy in more ways than one. They helped fashion the personality of one of the most eccentric figures of his age, a man whose inner complexities continue to intrigue all who read his works, who learn the strange details of his life, or who try to scythe through the thickets of his imaginings. The man who created the Red Queen, the Snark, the Mad Hatter, and Tweedledum and Tweedledee is a figure whose character perpetually demands explanation. His time in the parsonage on Morphany Lane seems at the very least a reasonable place to start.

During his eleven years in Daresbury, one of his early biographers wrote, the young Charles "made pets of odd and unlikely animals" (snails, worms, and toads, mainly), "invented strange diversions for himself" (such as creating a back-garden railway out of wheelbarrows and barrels, and offering rides to his siblings—but only on condition that they accede to a long list of strange and ridiculous regulations he had invented to make their journeyings from shrubbery to shrubbery ever more bizarre), and persuaded his father to instruct him in the theory and practice of logarithms. (It speaks to the intellectual tenor of the times that an Anglican minister assigned to an obscure and austere rural village in northern England could be assumed to have the capacity to teach his son the intricacies of algebra; certainly, it speaks to the kind of peculiar intellectual grounding that would later serve Dodgson so very well.)

It was also a time when first evolved—despite a persistent vocal hesitation that some likened to a stammer, and despite a steadily increasing deafness in his right ear, brought about by a childhood attack of mumps—what would be his social qualities. His immense, long-lived, and excessively clever family first saw to that: his relationships with each of his seven sisters—Fanny, Elizabeth, Caroline, Mary, Louisa, Margaret, and Henrietta—and his three brothers—Edwin, Wilfred, and Skeffington—were warm, and prepared the outwardly quiet and rather piously high-minded Dodgson for a lifetime of close associations and lasting friendships.

However, it is worth noting that only three of his siblings ever married—two of the boys (Wilfred and Skeffington) and only one of the girls (Mary). So the young Charles was brought up in an atmosphere in which familial solicitude was tinged with a strong sense of independence, solitude, and self-reliance. The fact that he himself never married either, but developed intimate friendships with many, most notably among them dozens of young children whose innocence must have so reminded him of the idylls of his Daresbury childhood, becomes to those who remain intrigued by the conundrum (and there are many amateur psychiatrists all) promptly more understandable, if not necessarily entirely explicable.

That so many of the women in his books were strong and cruel also puzzles many. His mother, Frances, was agreeable and kind, so we must suppose that the housemaids she employed—recorded in Charles's diaries as being mostly fat, arrogant, and generally disagreeable—provided the models.

Not that Charles was the only unusual one of the Dodgson children. His youngest brother, Edwin, chose to become a missionary to Tristan da Cunha, an island pinioned in the windswept isolation of the south Atlantic; and his youngest sister, Henrietta, lived to a great age, also beside the sea, with a vast collection of cats—having previously traveled around England carrying a portable stove that allowed her to cook her beloved sausages in the privacy of her various bedrooms. She also once mistakenly took an alarm clock to church with her, instead of a Bible, with predictably catastrophic results. But the children Charles Dodgson took with him when he visited this old lady in her Brighton home were enchanted by her, in part because they said that she reminded them so much of Charles. He was, already, something of an odd duck, if not necessarily the oddest.

The idylls of Cheshire came to an end, however, when in 1843—with Charles now eleven years old—his father won the elevation he had long supposed his due: Robert Peel, the prime minister, appointed him to the rectorship of the parish of Croft-on-Tees, a parish one hundred miles to the north and east of Daresbury. There was more responsibility, a bigger house, more money—and eventually a slew of other ecclesiastical preferments, all in north Yorkshire, which included the jobs of examining chaplain to the bishop of Richmond, the archdeaconry of Richmond, and finally, the summit of his career, the canonry of Ripon Cathedral.

Young Charles, the eldest son of a man of now steadily rising stature in England's established church, would for the next decade be schooled and groomed accordingly. This was the time when Victorian culture would try to forge the boy into muscular manhood, to transform him into a creature both noble and genteel. But it was a plan that failed, signally, and Dodgson's Yorkshire years instead helped impress upon this curious and sensitive boy a pattern of living that was markedly different from those of most others around him. This is the time when we can perhaps first discern the origins of his lifelong fascination with very young girls—the period in his life that would lead, inexorably, to the friendships that would culminate in the writing of his literary masterpiece.

After initially being taught at home—school was not compulsory in those days—he was sent away, once his father had sufficient funds, to the more formalized forcing-house of a boarding school. For the first two of his teenage years he was educated locally, at a small private school in the town of Richmond. There were no reports that he was homesick there, or that he was bullied or unhappy. He liked his schoolmates, he did not care much for sports, and he quite welcomed the almost anarchic atmosphere of the place. He adjusted reasonably well, in other words—and swiftly became accustomed to the rather monastic life in an all-male boarding establishment.

But then, in 1846, he was sent down south, to the Rugby School. There he encountered a very different world, one, as he admitted later in life, that he cordially and eternally loathed. It is fair to say that the Rugby which the fourteen-year-old Dodgson attended was a far more kindly and less brutal establishment than it once had been—Thomas Arnold (father of Matthew) had seen to that during his time as headmaster, which had ended just four years beforehand. But it was still a place of testosterone-fueled excess—regular bullying, the widespread use of corporal punishment, the system of intensely violent sporting competition, the continued use of smaller boys as the "fags" or personal servants of upperclassmen—and Dodgson made no secret of his abhorrence of its excesses. That said, he was no shrinking violet. One of his early biographers, his nephew Stuart Collingwood, noted that "even though it is hard for those who have only known him as . . . gentle and . . . retiring . . . to believe it, it is nevertheless true that, long after he left school his name was remembered as that of a boy who knew well how to use his fists in defense of a righteous cause," by which one assumes the writer meant the protection of smaller boys.

Indeed, he came to love and admire the very notion of childhood innocence during his three years at Rugby. One of his more recent biographers insists that his time at Rugby "revolted his sensitive nature"—for not only did he recoil from the bullying and flogging and fagging, not only did he instinctively offer a protective shroud to those who were tormented or harassed (which, presumably, included the more-or-less-meaningless teenage sexual abuse that afflicted all British boarding schools of the time), but he himself was mercilessly teased for his stammering and derided for his lack of interest in organized games (with rugby football, supposedly invented there, most popular of all).

He made it abundantly clear during his time at school that he was anything but a man's man. His adolescence does not seem to have been marked by any sexual activity at all (he kept no diary at Rugby, so we cannot be entirely sure)—and if he favored the company of younger children, and, in later years, the company of young girls, then it seems to have been because in them he discovered a kind of worshipful love and sensitivity and tenderness that was otherwise utterly lacking in the masculine world in which he was obliged to exist.

Why he never sought sanctuary in marriage is quite another matter; but his rejection of the roguish coarseness of the conventional world that he first sighted at school in Warwickshire was born in these late teenage years, and thereafter never left him. This was the time in his life when he was first tempted to seek sanctuary in the comfort of the crinoline, when lace and gay bonnets and fair young skin and idle chatter would start to mean far more to him than mud and muscle, sweat and sawdust.

He returned to this more favored kind of world each school holiday, of course, when he returned home to Yorkshire, and to his sisters. They and their friends would provide him with at least a simulacrum of what he so keenly needed, until he was to discover other sources a few years later.

Emotional longing was not the only side of Dodgson first defined at Rugby. His academic work was peerless—particularly in mathematics. His tutor, Robert Mayor, remarked in a letter to the Reverend Dodgson that he had not met a more promising boy at his age since coming to Rugby. His headmaster, the thin and sickly Archibald Tait, in time to be elevated to the Archbishopric of Canterbury, felt much the same. "His mathematical knowledge is great for his age, and I do not doubt he will do himself credit in the classics," he wrote. "His examination for the Divinity prize was one of the most creditable examinations I have seen." (There is a melancholy coda to the unfolding of Dodgson's long and respectful relationship with Archbishop Tait. As headmaster of Rugby,

Tait was both a teacher and a mentor to Dodgson. In his appearance and demeanor he was not unlike his pupil: he was shy and intellectual and perpetually unwell, having been born crippled and obliged to wear leg braces all his life—which may well have had a bearing on Dodgson's later outlook. In the spring of 1856, a month-long outbreak of scarlet fever took five of the Taits' seven children, all of them little girls. The nation, from Queen Victoria down, was moved to stunned silence by this awful event. Dodgson was keenly aware of the tragedy that had beset his old headmaster: he would have thought it unusually cruel for even the kindest deity to rob the Reverend Tait of so many small girls.)

Then again, the literary ingenuity and curiously bizarre wit that, mixed with a keen interest in mathematics and astronomy and symbolic logic, would underpin his intellectual leanings seem also to have been conceived around this time. Not only did Dodgson become something of a performer, at least at home—dressing up as Aladdin and doing conjuring tricks, or performing puppet plays in a homemade marionette theater—but he began to edit and distribute small domestic magazines, to write poems, to produce elegant and amusing line drawings—all adumbrations of the remarkable gifts that would propel him to worldwide prominence just a short while later.

His homemade magazines survive in archives. *Useful and Instructive Poetry* was first, and went through five monthly issues; the half dozen issues of the *Rectory Magazine*, which coincided with his Rugby days, lives in an air-conditioned vault in Austin, Texas. With their limericks, puzzles, essays, poems long and short, satires, wild puns, railway riffs, ballads, strange observations, lays, burlesques, and a host of illustrations of scrupulous complexity, both publications hint powerfully at the talent to come.

It is difficult to imagine a schoolchild having so frantic and creative a mind.

After he escaped from Rugby—"I cannot say that I look back upon my life at public school with any sensation of pleasure, or that any earthly considerations would induce me to go through my three years again," he wrote six years later, in his diary—he went up to Oxford, to the city and university where he would spend the remainder of his life. He would make just one foray overseas—to France and Russia, in 1867—but otherwise, and for always, it was Oxford.

Forty years before, his father had taken a double first at Christ Church. Although precious little string-pulling would have been needed to assure a place in the same college for the young Dodgson—so intellectually gifted was he, so artistically unusual, and with such an obvious aptitude for the mathematics that Dr. Mayor rightly suspected would be his chosen subject—there can be little doubt that letters would have passed between the rural rector and the academic dean to make doubly certain that entrance was secure. And so it was: Charles Dodgson arrived at The House (as Christ Church was and still is familiarly known) to matriculate in 1851.

The beginning of his academic life was distinctly unpropitious. When first he arrived in the immense and sprawling Christ Church, he found it filled to bursting and no room available for him. He had thus to return to Yorkshire, to wait. Then a kindly friend of his father's who had a house in Oxford wrote to say he would welcome the boy in his own home. And so back south he traveled (by stagecoach: the railway train was still new and unfamiliar, and had only just uncoiled itself along the Thames Valley up to Oxford). But within just two days of his settling in, an urgent message arrived for Dodgson from Yorkshire, demanding that he board the northbound coach once more and return to the rectory at Croft-on-Tees yet again. This time the reason was especially tragic. His mother, just forty-seven years old and with a family that included the exceptionally needy four-year-old Henrietta, had suddenly and unexpectedly died. A stroke, most probably, or meningitis—"inflammation of the brain"—had killed her within hours of Charles's leaving. Her sister Lucy stepped into the breach and would mother Charles's younger siblings for the next twenty-five years.

Though we cannot know exactly just how severe a shock his mother's passing truly was, since he had a custom of locking his miseries deep within and never committing his most melancholy thoughts to paper, the many references in his later published writing to the inestimable value of maternal love suggests that the loss was expectedly unbearable. But his demeanor was of the stoic: he never mentioned his grief, nor did his brief absence from college disrupt his studies in a significant way.

He returned to Oxford and fell in without demur with the traditions and customs of the institution. He was first given rooms in the cozily intimate Peckwater Quadrangle. He swore on his knees to uphold the Thirty-Nine Articles of the Church of England. He happily wore the cap and gown that were the undergraduates' proctorially enforced clothing—his cap with a black tassel, to distinguish him from the "tufts," the noblemen-undergraduates who wore gold—and he attended such lectures as he thought interesting and enlightening.

His affinity for scholarship placed him in something of a minority. Oxford in those days—a dirty, muddy, unkempt town of horses and dogs (scores of them running almost wild through the college cloisters) and high-spirited young swells sent there unwillingly as preparation for lives of indolence and privilege—was on one level not quite the sanctuary for cleverness that some of the other great universities of Europe were, nor indeed could it compare in scale of scholarship with Cambridge, which lay a mere one-day's diligence-ride away.

Oxford in those years was, at least on one level, a forcing-house for *flaneurs*—and Christ Church itself, run with lenient insouciance by the man known as "the Old Bear," the rather uninspiringly conservative classics dean Thomas Gaisford, was a distillation of all that was decadent and loutish about Oxford: there were immense drunken parties, outbreaks of wanton vandalism, and a code that dictated disrespect be meted out against authority, architecture, and the church in equal measure. One especially lively evening saw five hundred of the college's windowpanes smashed by roving bands of well-dined scholars, and the ancient walls of both Tom Quad and Peckwater smeared with graffiti of a language and tone that, for its surprisingly scatological profanity, still shocks.

Yet, of course, there was also quietude and academic distinction all around, and in marvelous abundance, even if so many of Dodgson's contemporaries chose to ignore and disdain it. Men of huge ability and world-shaking influence were at Oxford at the time—men such as Wellington, Peel, Gladstone, Ruskin, and the prime minister lords Salisbury and Rosebery, men whose intellectual rigor and later achievement knew few equals. Dodgson was a young man who was entirely inclined to learn from them.

Perhaps he did not quite follow Wordsworth's stern precepts of "plain living and high thinking," but he kept himself at some remove from the general boisterousness of his undergraduate colleagues—rising shortly after six each morning with tea brought to him by Brooks, his college scout; attending chapel twice a day; and making certain he got to all lectures exactly on time. At five o'clock dinner in the immense hall, he was known for keeping his own counsel, such that later memoirists confessed they never suspected that this quiet young man, known in his early months in college for his air of polite studiousness, would, in time, unleash upon the world works of great wit and imagination.

His prompt return from the misery of Yorkshire to a regime of high-octane study back at Oxford was duly rewarded just a year later, when he took his Honour Moderations examinations, and achieved an immediate First Class in mathematics (though he did rather less well in classics). A short while thereafter—and, somewhat curiously, before he had actually completed his degree—he was nominated for a *studentship*, the quaint term employed in Christ Church, then and still, for a fellowship. He would be given a grant of 25 pounds sterling a year, not required in any formal sense to work, and granted the right to remain in residence forever. The members of the Senior Common Room had clearly recognized in Dodgson a young man of exceptional talent and ability.

He was nominated to the studentship by a friend and former Christ Church contemporary of his father, the great Anglican traditionalist and Oxford Movement cofounder Edward Bouverie Pusey. Pusey was a man of very considerable influence in Oxford and beyond, one of a group of great intellectual divines that included Cardinal Newman, a former Anglican who famously turned Catholic (thereby excluding himself from any ambitions to be dean of the rigidly Anglican Christ Church himself, but whose later reward was to be beatified by the Vatican in 2010)—and the master of Balliol College, Benjamin Jowett, of whose intellect the undergraduates of the time cruelly remarked, "Here come I, my name is Jowett, There is no knowledge but I know it; I am the Master of this College; What I don't know just isn't Knowledge."

Though the backing of Dodgson had an unmistakable whiff of nepotism to it, and though Dodgson himself no formal degree at the time, the unadorned importance and imposing character of the Reverend Pusey trumped all other considerations, and Dodgson soon won his elevation, which secured him a room and rations for life. Dodgson did not exactly reciprocate, however. Although he remained steadfastly devout through all his years, he demurred at embracing Pusey's High Church and traditionalist leanings. He remained, by contrast, a member of a much broader churchly communion and did not support a return by Anglicans to the embrace of Catholic ritual and dogma, as was urged by Pusey and others in the Oxford Movement. This might have later resulted in some cooling of the relationship between himself and Pusey—though not, apparently, an outright breach.

Meanwhile, Dodgson did his best to attend to his studies, knowing he had something of a responsibility to acquire the good degree that Pusey assumed he would, in time, attain. But there were so many distractions at Oxford, as generations of scholars before and since have come to know. By the time he was raised to his studentship, he was just twenty, a tall, gangly, floppy-haired, and blue-eyed young man. By now he was less diffident than in his first months. He was friendly, courteous, charming. He sang well, was an excellent mimic, told stories, played (and won) at games of charades. The slight hesitation in his speech, the body language he had to employ as one who was slightly deaf to hear those speaking to him, his appearance of an almost childlike unworldliness all conspired to present him as a vulnerable and fascinating figure, one whom women and girls found endlessly irresistible. And it was in this latter area of his social world that he was unable to reciprocate fully.

For he did indeed get his degree—heading the list of First-Class honours in mathematics—helping secure his appointment as a college lecturer in the subject. He did not, however, rise to the kind of academic brilliance to secure a university appointment. It was a college appointment only, and this, like the studentship he already enjoyed, came with restrictions. He was obliged in due course to take Holy Orders, and he was not permitted—under the rigid terms that were demanded in exchange for accepting a permanent studentship in college—to marry.

The pleasures of matrimony were permitted for the dean and chapter only; and although these rules were to be relaxed a few years later, they did initially require that students of Christ Church be pious and celibate, the senior collegiate body being composed exclusively of bachelor men.

Thus was Charles Dodgson's social world promptly and roundly circumscribed. Charming, adorable, and desirable though he might be to Oxford's small platoons of eligible women, he could now make no formal union, secure no family for himself, never enjoy the circles of his own innocent children, like those among whom he had enjoyed so profoundly delightful a time back up in Daresbury, or up at the rectory in Croft. By the time the restrictions were eased and students permitted to marry, Dodgson himself had fallen into the habits of permanent bachelordom. He had succumbed to the rules of what was the polar opposite of a Faustian deal: he had sold his soul to Christ Church, and by doing so had denied himself the full flowering of a life on which, during his undergraduate years, he had teetered so temptingly on the brink.

So now it was time for him to invent a wholly new life, one lived on an entirely different plane, and in a manner that for the next quarter century would adroitly accommodate both his whims and beliefs and those of his collegial brothers. He turned to writing first, and by way of this swiftly evolving skill, and in more senses than one, he was reborn. Three things befell Charles Lutwidge Dodgson in the years immediately following his attainment of a degree and a college lectureship, and all of them were epiphanic. And all took place in Oxford in the warming spring days of 1856.

Chapter Three

MATTERS ARISING

THE FIRST OF THE EPIPHANIES HAD TO DO WITH A MAGAZINE that for some inexplicable reason (since it had nothing to do with either railways or wedding dresses) was called the *Train*.

Dodgson had been writing for some while. (He had also for years been a writer of prodigiously long letters. The pages and pages that he wrote to his sister Elizabeth had become a running joke in the family.) His enthusiasm for creating his own homespun family newspapers—and a curious scrapbook that he called *The Mischmasch*, now to be found at the Houghton Library at Harvard—had encouraged him to try his hand at contributing to popular literary journalism.

His first published poems—very juvenile—appeared in the *Oxonian Advertiser* in 1854, and a year later there were two slightly more successful attempts, a poem titled "The Lady of the Ladle" and a fanciful story that he called "Wilhelm von Schmitz," which were published in his family's local paper the *Whitby Gazette*. There was no signature under the Oxford efforts; there was in the Yorkshire paper—which thus is historically significant for publishing the first works by Dodgson that were clearly and identifiably his. However, he signed them "BB," initials he had also employed, mysteriously, in the *Rectory Magazine* some while before.

But then there appeared on the horizon a selection of new magazines, newspapers, and journals that, even if they turned out to be more ephemeral than the local versions, were winning popular attention, both in London and nationally. There was the *Comic Times* first, and the *Train* a little later. Both were the brainchildren of Edmund Yates, a flamboyant journalist and literary entrepreneur, a man whose enthusiasms were supported by his marriage into the fabulously wealthy Wilkinson family, their fortune deriving from swords and, in later times, razor blades. Yates started the *Times*, a magazine with a keen sense for the ridiculous, and he was happy to publish—though not to pay for—a scattering of Dodgson's submissions, particularly if they were inventive and fantastic. Though the weekly lasted for only sixteen issues, there were five contributions from this mysterious Oxford don who styled himself "BB." One of the pieces was a curious drama that he called *Photography Extraordinary*.

So the *Comic Times* collapsed, but Yates bounced back swiftly, and the first issues of the replacement monthly the *Train*—same staff, same offices, same money—appeared at the end of 1855. Dodgson sent in material for consideration right away. One piece was readily accepted for publication in the issue slated for March 1856—a small poem entitled *Solitude*. Yates received it warmly, except that he demanded one important change: no longer could Dodgson write under pseudonymous initials. Yates wanted it made clear to readers that new spirits were being harnessed for his new venture, and Dodgson had to select a new name.

And so he did. Writing from his Oxford rooms, he promptly proposed a selection of possibilities. The name *Dares*, perhaps—from the village of his birth, Daresbury. Yates said no. How about (for no apparent reason) *Edgar Cuthwellis?* Yates again declined, as he did to the variant *Edgar U. C. Westhill.*

Then Dodgson submitted a name that had some recognizable logic to it. He took his own first name, Charles, Latinized it to Carolus, and then re-Anglicized this to Carroll. He performed much the same trickery to his second name, his mother's family name Lutwidge, rendering it first to Louis. Louis Carroll. Yates pricked up his ears. *Maybe*, he said. *Almost. Have another go.* So Dodgson tried again. He changed the spelling from the continental "Louis" to the more English-looking "Lewis." *Lewis Carroll.*

To this Edmund Yates finally said yes. And so the March 1856 issue of the *Train* went to press with the small and relatively undistinguished poem "Solitude" published in a prominent position—above the byline of an entirely new author with an entirely manufactured name. Lewis Carroll had been officially born, and the world would under its impress eventually shift, if slightly, on its axis.

And while Charles Lutwidge Dodgson would eventually pass away, forty-two years after this moment of conception, the Lewis Carroll that was first to write in that untidy London magazine office in March 1856 is still very much alive today, and will probably live on forever.

———

Two other epiphanies would then occur to Mr. Carroll, writer, and in quick succession.

Dean Gaisford of Christ Church had died the year before, in June. He had been, as we've seen, a deeply conservative, retiring figure, an ancient divine steeped in the study of classics and unaware of any pressing need to alter the ways of his ancient college. The man who seemed likely to succeed him, a classicist, too, and one of world-class reputation, was, however, a man possessed both of a rationalist view of religion and a zeal for reforming academia. Doctrinal conservatives—such as Dodgson's sponsor, Edward Pusey—shuddered at the thought.

Their apprehension was well placed, for just five days after the passing of Gaisford, a man they had affectionately called the Old Bear, it was a forty-four-year-old Christ Church alumnus and high-flyer, who at the time was presiding as headmaster of Westminster School in London, who was ordered back to Oxford to take charge of the House: Henry George Liddell.

It was an appointment that was greeted with cheers in the House of Commons, and with fears among the ecclesiastical old guard of Oxford. It was also an appointment that would set in train a series of reforms and expansions that would place Christ Church firmly on the world map as an oasis of social and academic excellence (and, by chance, the Oxford college with the best-laid drains. Dean Liddell had an enduring fascination with matters of drainage and sewage and was determined to bring those at Christ Church up to standard. A visiting German admirer once arrived in Christ Church Meadow looking for the great man, to be told by a college servant that he "had just gone down the drain." He heard a cry from the bottom of an open hole and then saw the majestic head and mane of the scholar, stained with mud and running with sweat, emerging from the earth like a mole.)

Liddell came back to Oxford with a reputation for scholarship: along with Robert Scott he had edited the *Greek–English Lexicon*, which remains in print today, one of the great canonical books of the libraries of the learned. Dodgson himself had bought a copy back in 1848. The letter to his father asking for permission to lay out the necessary sum for such an awe-inspiring book survives; his father, who had known Liddell well, naturally gave immediate consent.

However, most crucially for the future life and career of Charles Dodgson, Dean Henry Liddell did not simply overawe the young mathematics lecturer with his intellect and his Olympian presence. The one fact about Liddell that came to count for most in Dodgson's life was that, above all else, the dean was a contented and liberally minded family man.

Liddell was of patrician stock himself—his uncle was a baron, his mother was the niece of an earl—and Ruskin noted admiringly that he was "one of the rarest types of nobly-presenced Englishmen." He then married well—to the statuesque, dark-haired, and somewhat imperious East Anglian beauty Lorina Hannah Reeve—forfeiting his Christ Church studentship in the process (something that Dodgson could have done, of course, had he ever decided to become betrothed). But marriage did not, of course, prevent Liddell from returning to the college as a dean. Indeed, most deans did marry, with Liddell's predecessor Gaisford doing so twice.

When the Liddells eventually arrived in Oxford, late in 1855, to take up residence in the deanery—"I am the Dean, and this is Mrs. Liddell," wrote a satirist some years later, in *Vanity Fair*, "She is the first and I the second fiddle"—they came with children. There was a son named Henry (whose brother Arthur had died during a scarlet fever outbreak at Westminster School); a daughter named Lorina Charlotte, after her mother; a babe-in-arms, Edith; and, at three years old, the unrivaled star of the small ménage, a pretty and uncommonly interesting little girl, Alice. There were to be four further sons born—though only three surviving—and two more daughters. But to contemporary history, Alice Liddell is the child who remains *prima inter pares.*

Dodgson first met the dean himself in January of 1856. On returning from the Christmas vacation with his family in Yorkshire, he had settled back to his tutoring routines at Christ Church and within a few days made a formal call on Liddell to ask if he might arrange a series of public lectures. No doubt he was charmed by the dean's trace of a northern accent—Croft was none too far from the Tyneside estate in Gateshead, where the Liddells had their seat, and Dodgson would have been familiar with the unique manner of local speech, and probably nostalgic upon hearing it in the otherwise very southern English surroundings of an Oxford college. Liddell happily agreed to Dodgson's plan: public lecturing, he told the young tutor, was a capital idea.

One day in the middle of the following month, Dodgson happened to stroll down from the college along the tree-lined Broad Walk that marches south across Christ Church Meadow and to the River Isis. All was delightful mayhem: taking place on that particular day on the river were the Hilary Term bumping contests for clinker-built rowing eights known as Torpids. It was a pleasant way to spend an afternoon—watching the young students milling about on the ice-cold river, the spectators eventually heading home for tea and crumpets by the fire.

On this particular day he encountered for the first time some of the Liddell family: Mrs. Liddell, her sister, and the two eldest children, Henry and Lorina—or Harry and Ina, as they were generally known. He was instantly enchanted. Mrs. Liddell—for whom schoolboys at Westminster had displayed the same kind of fevered longing shown to Greer Garson's Mrs. Chipping—he found daunting, but rather magnificent. Harry, he declared to his diary a few days later, was "the handsomest boy I ever saw," and he happily "made friends" with him. Two days later, at a party, he fell similarly under the spell of Ina, and took the opportunity, as he also wrote, of making friends with her as well.

But the greatest delight was to occur a full academic session later, at the beginning of those dreamy days of an Oxford Trinity Term.

On Friday, April 25, Dodgson and a new-made friend, Reginald Southey, a medical student and a nephew of the poet Robert Southey, went together to the deanery garden. There they found for the first time all three Liddell girls—Lorina once again, baby Edith, and, this time, the three-year-old Alice.

It was a moment Dodgson was both to recognize and memorialize. "I mark this day," he would later write, once having succumbed to the astonishing charms of three-year-old Alice Liddell, "with a white stone."

The reason that Dodgson and Southey had gone to the deanery garden on that spring Friday involves the third of the three epiphanies that enveloped the young man.

The first was that he had been given a nom de plume and was on the brink of a new career. The second was that he had met and befriended the young lady who would be the central focus of his life for the coming years, and would provide him the name with which he would be forever associated; and now there was this third: he and Reginald Southey were friends because of their shared interest in a new and fast-developing art. Both young men—one a mathematician, the other a physician—were *photographers*.

Their main reason for going to the deanery garden that Friday afternoon was to see if they might make photographic studies of the Cathedral Tower. Just a few days beforehand, Dodgson had traveled down to London to buy his first camera; and this Friday, when he uncased his new-fangled apparatus of mahogany, brass, and expensive optics and prepared to try it out, happened also to be the very first time he met Alice Liddell.

So the trinity was now in place: Lewis Carroll, Alice Liddell, and a large folding box camera, all together, and in a pretty springtime garden hidden away in the separate and cloistered world at the center of the University of Oxford.

Chapter Four

THE RUDE MECHANICALS

CHARLES DODGSON HAD ORDERED HIS CAMERA IN LONDON, AT A
shop named Ottewill & Company, at 24 Charlotte Terrace, off the
Caledonian Road in Islington.

He had been introduced the year before to this new form of
art—a *black art*, some of the more suspicious called it, but, as it
turned out, for more specifically chemical reasons, given that it
stained its practitioners' hands—by his uncle Robert Skeffington
Lutwidge. Skeffington was a bachelor barrister who held a position
that had great incidental importance to Dodgson's development:
he was a Commissioner in Lunacy, a member of a panel of appointed government officials who had the responsibility of oversight for
the country's asylums, and for the formal determination of the
degrees of madness which compelled some sufferers to enter them.

The job necessarily brought Skeffington into intimate contact
with some of the community's more interestingly challenged and

unusually deranged men and women. Doubtless he would have spoken of his encounters with his young academically inclined nephew. And thus the pair would converse, as they made what Skeffington had decided would be photographic expeditions around the homestead in Croft, during which they took pictures (with admittedly only modest success) of the local bridges and cottages and the church where Charles's father preached.

It turned out to be a very heady mixture—the use of cameras and the talk of madness—for the younger man. The effect of the conversations about insanity and perverse imaginings may well have lingered long. But in the short term Charles became swiftly hooked by Skeffington's enthusiasm for the camera—and indeed he soon recognized a curious and unexpected harmony between the new art and the anecdotes that his uncle brought him from the madhouse.

For photography had a kind of manageable madness to it. There was, for example, the slightly crazy upside-down-ness of it all, the sight of the inverted image on the ground-glass screen, the now entirely different meanings of left and right, the bizarre concepts of *focus* and *out of focus*. In particular, he was wide-eyed at the darkroom conjuring tricks by which chemistry, a discipline of logic and order, was employed to create images out of the very air—or so it seemed, and the still further use of this same science to keep these new-made images fixed for all time, and with no ready explanation for why. Photography presented an almost unimaginable new magic—and there can be no doubt that these Yorkshire walks taken with his enigmatic uncle had a lasting effect on Dodgson's later creative energies.

All this started to combine during that summer—anecdotes about strange people, stories of madness and the attempts to cure it, and the making of imagery by the employment of both the precisions of science and the magical indisciplines of art. These things were set to marinate in Dodgson; and they did so while he was learning the tools of an entirely new occupation, one that would lead him, in just a short while, to the singular object of his creative desires.

Photography had other, more practical, enchantments for Dodgson. He had an aptitude for drawing; and though his technique was acceptable and interesting, he well knew he was not an especially talented draughtsman. Photography, with its limitless possibilities for documentary of a most precise and accurate kind, seemed to him to offer a ready alternative. He could record his impressions of people—especially through portraiture, which he cherished—with total accuracy and relative ease. The human hand might have been best at offering up subjective impressions; photography, by contrast, could produce impressions that were entirely objective, subject only to the whims and tinkering of he who crouched behind the lens.

It was all so very new. The ancients had known that certain chemicals darkened on exposure to light, the more so the more light falling upon them; and devices that could capture an image and then with lenses or mirrors divert it had been around for centuries. Yet it was not until the first half of the nineteenth century that Joseph Nicéphore Niépce and Louis Daguerre hit upon the idea of coating some surface with a light-sensitive substance and having an image diverted briefly onto the coated flatness. Such a procedure, they found, would result in a record of the light-created image, a record that could perhaps endure permanently, to be examined and to prompt pleasure and amazement long after the moment of its capture had passed.

Soon after this realization the machine that would perform this task came, the *camera*—the word means literally a vault, since it was within it that the light was captured and compelled to perform. It was a device that could be employed to absorb and divert an image—a view from a window, say, such as Nicéphore Niépce had captured with his crude camera on countless occasions in the late 1820s—and then preserve that image, to be looked upon at nighttime, say, when the view from the window had become quite obscured by darkness. The very moment that the public first saw such an image, it realized its significance. The new art took off from its standing start with the lightning speed of a gazelle.

Niépce's actual technique was cumbersome and grubby and most un-gazelle-like. His choice of location was his country house, named le Gras, deep in the countryside of the Bourgogne. He lugged his enormous homemade camera up to the top floor and positioned it by the window. His plan was to point it out of the window and let it absorb into its innards as much light as the French countryside was able to produce.

Others were experimenting around the same time. Most were chemists, and most favored the use of light-sensitive silver compounds as a means of capturing the illuminated images. Niépce chose not to employ silver for his work. Rather, he made use of a kind of bitumen, a naturally occurring tarry substance employed today in road-building, which Niépce knew would not much darken on exposure to light but would instead become hard and immalleable.

His pioneering plan for creating the world's first example of light-writing—which is what the word "photograph" means—sounds today more than a little bizarre. He would first coat the flat surface on which he would expose the images—a piece of tin, perhaps, or hammered pewter—with a layer of bitumen. He found that the thickness of the tar made it all but impossible to create a layer that was both flat and smooth. He therefore decided to dissolve his bitumen in lavender oil, and then drizzled the rather less viscous liquid carefully onto a hammered plate (pewter became his base of choice). He then placed this sticky plate inside and at one end of his wooden light-vault, his camera, which he had already arranged so that its shuttered eye, at the other closed end of the box, could gaze upon the view from his top-floor window. (An earlier experiment involved taking a picture of a table laid for dinner, though it seems not to have survived.)

He then removed the shutter that closed off the eye and left it off for something like nine hours, allowing the inside of the box to be filled with the varying degrees of light from the scene outside from dawn to dusk (and producing some interesting solar patterns on the resulting picture). Eventually he would decree that sufficient light had fallen on the tar-and-oil mixture to create an image composed not from lightness or darkness, but from the ridges and whorls of light-inspired hardness and softness that now lay on the pewter plate like a large-scale fingerprint. At this point he would close the lens again, remove the pewter plate from the camera, and wash it in yet more lavender oil—this time to remove the softer portions of the tar that had not been so affected by all the hours of exposure to the glare.

The result was a picture, of sorts. *The View from the Window at le Gras*, now housed in an argon-filled display case in Texas, needs to be seen at an angle, and in very low light. But once the eye adjusts, an image can be seen: coping stones, outbuildings, the shapes of trees, the vague suggestion of a distant landscape, and, in the foreground, more definite and precise, many examples of the edges of things.

It is the oldest extant photograph in the world. And it was taken in the summer of 1826—six years before Dodgson was born. Those six years saw advance upon advance. Niépce formed a brief commercial alliance (it was necessarily brief, for he died soon afterward, coincidentally on Charles Dodgson's first birthday) with a theatrical designer and diorama-maker named Louis Daguerre, who had independently developed a quite different (and seemingly very much cleaner) technique. Daguerre was a believer in the suitability of silver compounds—specifically silver iodide— that changed their appearance on exposure to light. He experimented with covering a thin metal plate in this material, exposing it to the scene he wished to record, then wafting the exposed plate through a cloud of mercury vapor, and finally washing the now amalgam-covered plate in salts that permanently fixed the resulting photographic image.

This technique, once perfected, offered up in time the famous daguerreotype that, during its brief ten years of popularity, left a canon of exquisite and haunting images that fascinate still. The first image made (in 1838) of a human being—a fellow having his boots shined on the Boulevard du Temple in Paris, unmoving while others—too elusive for the exposure—shift past him is but one of a thousand famous daguerreotypes still preserved.

Samuel Morse (he of the code) carried the technique to the United States, and a wild craze for formal portraiture swept the country, with Lincoln and Edgar Allan Poe among the subjects, these pictures being the first known of each, and offering a window into a world hitherto only reconstructed by those who could draw, or engrave, or paint.

The daguerreotype would have proved a truly universal phenomenon (for the French government bought the patent and offered it to the whole world for free) had not Daguerre decided for some unexplained reason to retain the patent to his process in England and to charge hefty license fees for anyone wishing to employ it. A competitor, a minor Wiltshire aristocrat named William Fox Talbot—who went by the name of Henry—was spurred into action and in 1843 came up with a quite different way to make a picture. The process was similar to Daguerre's in that it also employed the light-capturing properties of silver iodide—but it made what was to be called a *calotype* by fixing the image onto sheets of waxed paper rather than hammered metal—a method that offered very significant improvements on Daguerre's process. The two techniques then battled for supremacy among the fast-growing following of the art, each process eventually attracting two very different segments of photographic society.

The differences in appearance and presentation were crucial. No less an authority than Queen Victoria managed to understand the distinction. She wrote that it had been "Daguerreotypes and photographs" that she inspected at the Great Exhibition of 1851, where both kinds of images were on display; and though Her Majesty discerned only the outward differences—the sharp little framed daguerreotypes made on metal and protected by glass, the slightly blurrier calotypes on paper and pinned to the wall—there were subtler distinctions.

First, while Daguerre, using sheets of copper or tin, could make only one super-sharp and very delicate little image at a time, Talbot could reproduce from the sensitized paper (on which was what would henceforward be called the photographic *negative*) as many positive prints as he wished. And second, Talbot (who was also erroneously known by a hyphenated addition of his middle name, Fox-Talbot) placed the license fees he charged for his patented process at a very much lower level than did the Frenchman his, and waived them altogether for those "photographers," as they would eventually be named, who he decided were not professionals.

So while Daguerre's elegant and scrupulous methods appealed to the studio portraitist and assured that the daguerreotype would be the preferred activity of the trade, Talbot's methods attracted the educated classes. His paper-print invention spawned a hobby that soon captured hearts and minds across a wide swath of Britain's polite society and ensured that photography had progressed from conception to maturity to a nationwide obsession before Charles Dodgson had left Rugby School.

Photography swiftly became almost a tribal pursuit in Britain, intriguing the gentry and the landed (though not the über-aristocracy, who retained their traditional interests in painting and hunting). An immense number of well-off, clever people were intrigued by this exciting new technology—one into which people, with their freshly taken photographs exchangeable overnight by way of the newborn postal system, could gain easy entry into a universe of art and creativity, together with a ready-made network of like-minded enthusiasts with whom to share success and failure, and from whom to seek advice and support.

The amateur photographer was thus born of the calotype's success. Soon thereafter, there sprang up a magazine of that name, the most revered and ancient chronicle of the craft, which still flourishes in London. Photographic books—precursors of today's coffee-table volumes—then started to appear, with Talbot's *Pencil of Nature*, published in 1844, being the first.

In 1856, with his springtime visit to Mr. Ottewell's emporium on Charlotte Terrace, Charles Dodgson—who was the perfect type-specimen of the demographic, being fairly well born, exceptionally clever, and a member of a *corps d'élite* of intelligentsia—eagerly and excitedly joined their ranks.

Yet, as it happened, Dodgson chose to employ neither the calotype nor the daguerreotype technique to make his own pictures. He selected—after taking advice from Uncle Skeffington, and from his clever medical colleague at Christ Church, Reginald Southey—a third and very new method. Called the *wet-plate collodion process*, this extension of each of the first two methods was also developed in the 1850s, just as Dodgson was going up to Oxford.

The invention of the calotype might have fascinated the educated classes, and first inspired Dodgson's own fascination, but collodion turned a hobby for the elite into a pastime for the masses. In short, collodion democratized Victorian photography.

It is a melancholy reality that the collodion method was first perfected by a man who has now quite vanished, at least compared to both Daguerre and Talbot, and yet who produced what was truly a watershed in the development of photography. Frederick Scott Archer was the second son of a Hereford butcher, and by inclination and profession neither a chemist nor a photographer, but a numismatist and sculptor. It was his need to advertise his work that led him to photography.

Archer decided that the best way to get new commissions was to show potential customers faithful images of his sculpture. For an artist as little known as he was, it would be far better to attract people in this way than to require that they come to his studio. Moreover, sculpture was well suited to being photographed: a large piece of hewn marble or limestone or a casting in bronze was generally disinclined to move, and so would not mind the lengthy exposure times that Daguerre's and Talbot's methods required. Archer's thought to use photography to get the word out by this means was a small stroke of genius.

However, there were two specific technical problems. First of all, Talbot's calotypes did not have enough resolution to reveal the full delicacy and intricacy of his carvings. And second, it was impossible, or at least it was profoundly difficult, to create more than a single daguerreotype at a time, undermining the whole point of his using photography as a means of advertising his work. An improved process—one that offered high resolution and the opportunity to create many editions—would serve him better; and if the two giants in the field were unable to create such a process, he would simply try to do so himself.

The solution to his problem emerged, improbably, by way of the British Army's field hospitals and an invention that came about as a result of a kitchen accident in Switzerland.

The accident happened in 1846, when a chemist named Schönbein, who was somewhat ill-advisedly conducting experiments where he usually made his lunch, knocked over a vial of concentrated nitric acid, and wiped up the puddle with a nearby piece of cotton cloth, said to have been an apron. He then hung the apron on the door of the oven, and a few minutes later, having dried, the apron exploded with a bang and a brilliant flash, leaving nothing behind.

Schönbein had made what was later to be called *guncotton*, or *nitrocellulose*, a high explosive that, when mixed with a variety of other things, would become the core component of some of warfare's most enduring weapons.

The mixture of acids and cellulose—whether that cellulose is cotton or wood or horse chestnuts makes no difference—can produce a variety of substances within the nitrocellulose family. One kind is used as film stock—nitrate film, which despite its exceptional flammability, was used for decades in cinemas and the X-ray rooms of hospitals. But perhaps the most unusual member of the family is created when nitrocellulose guncotton is mixed with ether and alcohol—producing the viscous substance collodion.

This new substance was found to dry quickly into a clear and thin film, a coating that was both elastic and lasting. In 1848 it was adopted by doctors across Europe as an ideal substance for dressing wounds: it behaved like a new piece of skin, it kept out damp and infection, it was flexible, and it seemed to have some kind of healing properties. It seemed, particularly to Florence Nightingale's nurses in Crimea, an almost magical discovery, and was immediately and widely used for the treatment of soldiers suffering battlefield injuries. It is still sold today, and many is the mother who blesses collodion for the instant mending of children's grazes and skinned knees.

At the same time, a search was under way in the photographic world for some means whereby one might produce a number of positive images from the negative image captured by a camera and might have that image be both crystal-clear and sensitive to the subtleties of illumination of the subject. The daguerreotype was sensitive to subtlety, but only single images could be made. The calotype allowed several prints, but had low resolution and poor sensitivity to light. It was widely agreed that this means would be a thin and optically impeccable glass plate covered with silver iodide, but no one had thus far managed to come up with a substance that was transparent and would allow silver iodide to adhere to the glass.

A few bold experimenters tried albumen—egg white. It worked, but poorly, and only just. And then in 1851 Frederick Archer heard about collodion. He made a batch of it, mixed silver iodide into it, smoothed it thinly and carefully onto a glass plate, then placed it, still wet and tacky, into the back of his camera, and exposed it to light. Within just a few seconds—not the few minutes that the calotype process had always demanded—he saw that an image had indeed been acquired.

Moreover, the collodion–silver iodide mix turned out to be super-sensitive to light. Once the image had been prompted to appear fully, and by the application of further baths of chemicals had been persuaded to remain fixed and permanent, it was realized that this brand-new kind of photography was going to do just what the photographic community (and Mr. Archer) wanted. The images it created were produced quickly, accurately, and, in many other ways, near perfectly.

The wet-plate collodion process was thus invented—though Archer, never bothering to patent his invention (because, it is said, he never realized its significance) faded into obscurity and poverty. He died six years later, his wife the following year. The British Crown, which in time was made fully aware of the significance of Archer's invention, voted an annual pension to three otherwise destitute children, on the grounds, as the *Dictionary of National Biography* has it, "that their father had reaped no benefit from an invention which had been a source of large profits to others."

One of those others would be Charles Dodgson, though his profits—great as they might eventually be—would be more indirectly won. He embraced the collodion process enthusiastically— so enthusiastically, indeed, that some years later he wrote a poem about it, in the trochaic tetrameters employed so familiarly by Longfellow in his *Song of Hiawatha*:

> First a piece of glass he coated
> With Collodion; and plunged it
> In a bath of Lunar Caustic
> Carefully dissolved in water;
> There he left it certain minutes.
> Secondly my Hiawatha
> Made with cunning hand a mixture
> Of the acid Pyro-gallic,
> And the Glacial Acetic,
> And of alcohol and water;
> This developed all the picture.
> Finally he fixed each picture
> With a saturate solution
> Of a certain salt of soda . . .

This method already having been taught to Dodgson by his uncle, it remained for him only to buy his camera.

He had a little more money in the bank just now—his accounts at the Old Bank in the Oxford High Street (now a hotel of the same name) showed his receipts from his studentship, from a scholarship he had been awarded two years before, and from his mathematics lecturing. He could say with some satisfaction that, all told, at the end of 1855 he was earning three hundred pounds sterling a year, when the previous January he had made nothing and had lived quite penniless, aside from subventions from his family. But now he was in funds—though, like a typical Oxford academic, then as now, hardly rolling in cash. But in 1856, when he first asked Skeffington to inquire in the London shops about prices, he came to the eventual conclusion that he could afford, he thought, the fifteen pounds that Messrs. Ottewill charged for their best and most sophisticated machine. Since this kind of sum was what an average household yearly paid its senior servants, it was no trivial decision for Dodgson.

He dithered only a little. On Tuesday, March 18, he and Reginald Southey took the train to Paddington and made their way up to Islington, and to 24 Charlotte Terrace. Dodgson inspected the various models available, and finally plumped for the famous Double Folding camera for which the Ottewills were making themselves such a name. He also chose a lens, ground and polished by the equally distinguished (and gold-medal-winning) London lens-making firm of Andrew Ross & Co.; handed over the cash; and formally placed the order. Southey advised him that he also needed chemicals and the folding darkroom tent, and it seems likely that they went to the firm of R. W. Thomas in Pall Mall and handed over a very much smaller sum for an assortment of necessaries. And with that, the pair made their way back to Oxford, to await the eventual arrival of their trove of life-changing goods.

The choice of camera supplier was a good one, seen even at this remove. The business of Thomas Ottewill had been established in 1851 and, thanks to designs like the Double Folding camera, soon became one of the most successful British photographic manufacturers, contracted to make equipment for "the governments of England, India, Italy, Switzerland, the Colonies, etc.," according to a brochure. The model that Dodgson purchased won particular praise. The *Journal of the Photographic Society* said that there was no other design "which more fully combines the requisite strength and firmness with a high degree of portability and efficiency." To underline its suitability for the work, Ottewill's designed one specifically for Frederick Scott Archer, the inventor, of course, of the collodion process that it was created to employ.

The Thomas Ottewill Registered Double Folding camera was a thing of great beauty and precision, a triumph of the art. It was basically a pair of open-ended Spanish mahogany boxes, one with a lens, the other with a removable back for the light-sensitive plate, with one of the boxes slightly narrower than the other to allow it to move inside the larger. The progress of this movable part would be adjustable along a pair of brass tracks, one mounted on the underside of the smaller box, the other on the upper side of the Honduran mahogany baseboard. A knurled brass screw could advance or retard the box along the track, tooth by tooth, so that it slid in or out of the larger box—which was fixed to the baseboard—in order to change the focus. More lacquered brass fittings, a brass-bound f2.0 lens, a focus screen that could take a collodion plate up to ten inches by twelve inches across, and an elegant leather carrying-case. Models in good condition are rare today. At a recent camera sale at Christie's, an Ottewill of the same model and year as Dodgson's sold for twenty-five thousand dollars.

And this model had an additional convenience: its ingenious design made it highly portable. Both of the boxes that made up the bulk of the camera, if separated one from the other, could be made to collapse down to almost nothing, an elaborate system of brass hinges permitting the sides to fold down and then to be secured flat. There was the further advantage of having one collapsed box sufficiently smaller than the other: it could be slipped inside it. The entire camera, which was a good size—a couple of feet long and more than a foot wide and a foot high when ready for operation— could, when collapsed, be reduced to the size of a large sandwich.

A further stanza from Dodgson's *Hiawatha* parody describes the instant love affair in which he found himself upon seeing the instrument. The romance of the moment carried him slightly away, though, and he managed to get the wood wrong: Ottewill liked to use a pale kind of durable—if heavy—Spanish mahogany in making its machines, and an arboreally unsophisticated Dodgson was to draw his own, incorrect, idea of what the wooden case was made of. But it matters little, for this was love.

> From his shoulder Hiawatha
> Took the camera of rosewood
> Made of sliding, folding rosewood
> Neatly put it all together.
> In its case it lay compactly,
> Folded into nearly nothing;
> But he opened out the hinges,
> Pushed and pulled the joints and hinges,
> Till it looked all squares and oblongs,
> Like a complicated figure
> In the Second Book of Euclid.

The camera itself arrived in Oxford on May 1, 1856, in a large wooden crate. The chemicals and folding darkroom got there a little later, and porters lugged the assortment of containers across the quadrangles to Dodgson's rooms—whereupon he and Southey set to the delicious task of uncrating them, of removing the straw packing, and extracting the confection of shiny mahogany and brass and glassware, and then of assembling what needed to be assembled so that the famous camera was finally ready for use. It remained at first only to try it all out and then select a subject for the first photograph. "I am now ready," Dodgson wrote in his diary for May 13, "to begin my art."

It took some starting. The camera was one thing, relatively easy to set up and to use. But the chemistry of it all was tricky and could at first be most dispiriting—not least because so much of the process, both before the taking of the photograph and afterward, had to be undertaken in pitch dark. The photographer, before placing the camera and composing the shot, had to vanish inside his magical tent of mystery.

Moreover, whatever he then did inside his tent had to be done very quickly, especially if there was a sitter. If the pair were taking pictures of Christ Church Cathedral, which remained patiently immobile, they could afford to take their time; but almost from the very start, Dodgson had said he wanted to try his hand at portrait photography, so inspired had he been by the exhibitions he had seen in London.

And so the subject of the portrait—a living, breathing fidgeting human being—had to be there, in place, seated in a formal and fixed position, ready to be photographed, while the potions were mixed and the camera prepared. If the subject were an adult, the delay might present little problem. But to ask a child to remain seated while the photographer vanished inside his rather ominous-looking black tent would be something else entirely.

It was hot in Oxford in May 1856, and the stifling and airless atmosphere inside the tiny R. W. Thomas tent into which Dodgson had to scurry was compounded by the acrid aroma of the chemicals. Dodgson and Southey spent much of their time trying to make collodion plates, dribbling collodion from its storage bottle onto a piece of glass that had been cut, ten inches by eight, to fit inside the backplate of the camera.

The glass had to be perfectly clean, polished as a waiter might polish a champagne flute. The dribbling of the collodion had to be performed very gently, very carefully, and the liquid patted and shaken and smoothed down so that the resulting surface was optically flat. This was important, since any bulges or bubbles or bumps on the collodion's surface would alter the resulting focus; and the sharp precision of the collodion method was the very thing that so appealed to the fastidious Dodgson.

Once this had been accomplished—with the sitter still waiting patiently outside—then the loaded and very sticky plate would be dipped into a prepared bath of the light-sensitive silver-iodide mixture, with everyone making sure that no glimmer of light snuck its way into the tent to fog the plate before even the first exposure was made. Finally, the dripping and still tacky plate was loaded carefully into its brass frame—no errant cuff or curtain permitted to brush against it, no dust allowed to settle on it, no patches of dryness brought about by the plodding darkroom procedure—and the frame was inserted into the back of the camera.

Finally, Dodgson had to make quite sure that the brass cap was firmly in place and covering the lens (there was no shutter device on early cameras)—after which, and finally, the tent could be taken down or moved, light could be allowed to flood onto the scene, and the sweating occupants of the tent would emerge blinking back into the illuminated world, with the great wooden camera unveiled and ready to go to work.

The very first pictures the pair of them took were, not surprisingly, of one another. Each could be counted on to be as patient and long-suffering as was necessary while they learned their new craft. The procedure involved constant work, a choreography of patient and precise movement and flow, which they managed to accelerate as they learned. It went more or less as follows: Dodgson, on this occasion taking a photograph of Southey, would sit him before the lens, having prepared and inserted the plate as already described. He would next adjust his subject's pose, the lighting, the position of curtains, and the backdrop, and then step back to the Ottewill camera. Next, and with a dramatic flourish that said "Keep Absolutely Still!" he would remove the brass cap that covered the lens—and silence would fall on the room as the two men remained as utterly unmoving as humanly possible. In the early days it might take as long as forty-five seconds for the iodide to register the image—an excruciating period, though there was no need for the neck braces and tie-downs that prevented people moving as they were being captured for the exposures required for a daguerreotype or a calotype.

Once he finally replaced the cap—and once everyone could breathe again—Dodgson would extract the plate from the back of the camera—the glass now swiftly protected from the light by an ingenious flap—and take it into the darkness of the tent. Here he developed the image by washing it in a pyrogallic acid solution, a bottle of which he had prepared some while before; he would then wash it in water to halt further development, and fix it permanently by bathing it in a further solution of "hypo," or sodium thiosulphate. Then and only then would he reemerge into the daylight to see what had been wrought. (One thing he had invariably wrought was a black stain on his hands, the nearly indelible results of exposure to spills of the chemicals, the iodide especially. Not for nothing was photography widely known as the black art.)

Yet, whatever the result, it was still, of course, only a negative. To produce positive prints required still more labor of Dodgson: he would have to dry and varnish the negative by holding the plate before a fire, and then go through an entirely new ritual of producing a contact print on paper, developing and fixing it in just the same way as was done with the glass plate. But finally, an hour or so after he had first opened up the Ross lens to receive the forty-five seconds of light reflected from the nooks and crannies of Reginald Southey's face and form, there it would be, reproduced in black and white on a piece of stiff photographic paper, ready for the picture album, and for posterity.

Chapter Five

THE FIRST MAKINGS OF ART

THE FIRST IMAGES WERE RATHER POOR, TO THE SURPRISE OF neither man. Southey was the more experienced of the pair— he had been taking pictures for more than a year, had already produced an album, and had ignited sufficient enthusiasm in Dodgson for his friend to have begun the pastime the year before, had his income then allowed it.

The pictures that survive from the early summer of 1856 are thus nearly all the results of Southey's labors. All of them are portraits, each trimmed into neat and tiny shapes, usually oval, and mounted in albums now stored away at Princeton. There is a portrait of an unknown young Christ Church man, gazing thoughtfully into the camera; a self-portrait, with Southey looking to his left, with a similar expression of dreamy contemplation; and an image of Dodgson himself, the left half of his face in semi-profile, hair neatly pomaded but with curls cascading over his ears. His left hand is pressed against his cheek, emerging from a dark and over-sized sleeve that might be that of a smoking jacket, were one not aware that Dodgson abhorred smoking (and would leave the room if anyone lit a Lucifer or that kind of cheap clay pipe known as a churchwarden), and he is seated firmly against the back of a chair that appears to be covered in vivid and very un-Oxford-like tiger skin, so that the setting appears more bordello than academe. This is probably the earliest photographic glimpse we have of Dodgson, mathematics teacher, Anglican clergyman, and journeyman writer.

Southey produced one other photograph of significance to the story during those first few weeks of May. Dodgson managed to persuade the nine-year-old Harry Liddell to come over from the deanery to Southey's rooms to sit for a picture. The result was barely usable—Harry fidgeted too much for a good exposure—but it did afford the two the opportunity to go to see the dean and show him his son's image. Liddell was enchanted, and asked Dodgson to stay to lunch. Mrs. Liddell was, on this early occasion, even more delighted—though her enchantment toward Dodgson and his photography is reckoned to have diminished over subsequent years—and the children probably circled the pair with frantic requests of "Show me! Show me!" And there was the governess, Mary Prickett, who gazed with guarded admiration at the young scholar, so evidently a man of talent and romance.

The camera turned out to open all manner of doors for Dodgson—to the world of the deanery, to the Liddell family, and to a universe of good society, much of whose membership he would photograph over the coming years. He used the remaining weeks of that Trinity Term to consolidate his friendship with the dean's family. He took Harry boating, and then Ina—Lorina, named after her mother—came for a second expedition. Gradually and steadily, Dodgson became more aware that, much as he liked the company of his peers, he truly loved the company of children. Harry and Ina were to be the first of his friends; before long, there would be a small army of others, with the younger Liddell sisters—Alice and Edith—his favorites, very much in the van.

Yet it was quite another small girl—named Alice, too, but purely by coincidence—who was to be the first to benefit from Dodgson's growing skill with the camera. And she was living at the time not in Oxford, but in London.

———

Portraiture was what most interested Dodgson, and one assumes he began making images of people from the moment his skills had developed enough to allow him to assert his independence from Southey. His first attempts have not survived—but principally, most scholars think, because he was not satisfied with their quality, and, being a fastidious man, a perfectionist, he wanted his art to be worthy of posterity. There are just two presumed self-portraits from this time—one showing him standing by a table and looking down, which is held today in a library in Surrey, the second in the same pose but looking up, which is in the Morgan Library in New York. Both are catalogued in Dodgson's curiously blocky hand—and in his signature violet ink. They bear the numbers 15 and 16, suggesting there were many others that were either lost or discarded.

Once the long vacation of 1856 started, Dodgson was able to travel beyond Oxford, and he made the conscious decision to take along his camera, the folding darkroom and its chemicals, and all the other paraphernalia. There is some forensic suggestion—mainly from a paper trail of halfway reasonable portraits, some of his family and others of strangers—that he went first home, to

Croft. But the most important photographs from this period were taken when he arrived in the second week of June to stay at the house of his paternal uncle Hassard Hume Dodgson, in Putney.

Like Dodgson's maternal uncle Skeffington Lutwidge, Hassard Dodgson was a barrister, and the holder of another title of Victorian folderol—the Master of the Common Pleas. He was well connected and comfortably off, and lived in a mighty Victorian redbrick pile beside the Thames, Park Lodge. So Dodgson spent his two early summer weeks that year in an atmosphere of congenial relaxation, traveling occasionally into London to exhibits at the Royal Academy and the Society of Watercolourists, as well as visiting Sir Jonathan Pollock—to whom he would in time be distantly related by marriage. Pollock, who, in addition to being a council member of the newly constituted Photographical Society of London and a mathematician (a student of Fermat's theorem), was at the time one of England's leading judges, famous for his role in the interminable case of *Wright v. Tatham*, which many believe was the eight-year-long inspiration for *Jarndyce v. Jarndyce* in Dickens's great novel *Bleak House*. Dodgson went to see this formidable personage for advice: he returned entirely convinced that portraiture was to be his métier.

During those two June weeks he worked his way with great deliberation and assiduity through the entire range of subjects who lived in or turned up at Uncle Hassard's home. There was Hassard himself, then his wife, Caroline Hume, and an assortment of nephews and nieces and friends. Most of them were girls, whose names—Lucy, Laura, Charlotte, Amy, Katherine, and Millicent— far outnumbered those for boys.

One picture from that London interlude stands out: the one he took on the afternoon of June 19, 1856, of the four-year-old daughter of a senior civil servant who also served as the British emissary to Canada, Sir Thomas Murdoch. The Murdochs had heard of the photographic sessions under way in the drawing room over at Park Lodge and had seen some of the results. They wanted their four small children to be memorialized in collodion print by this charmingly shy and stammering Oxford parson, and so brought them round for tea.

Dodgson was immediately captivated by Alice Murdoch, a slightly chubby-cheeked little girl with long brown hair and an upturned nose. Her parents had clearly dressed her for the occasion, in a gingham smock with a lace collar and sleeves. Dodgson seated her on a high-backed chair of carved teak, then probably talked soothingly to her while he fussed with the chemicals, daubing them onto the glass slide—and finally, after tucking her legs up under her voluminous skirt so that she almost seemed to be perched without support on top of the chair's cushion, he bade her be still and took her picture. She remained perfectly still; in the resulting image her face is frozen, her mouth turned slightly down, every feature fixed with inexpressive resignation, displaying neither irritation nor joy, nor any of the many moods of childhood.

It is a portrait quite lacking in emotion, and it was judged severely for revealing too little communion between artist and subject, and for having an uneasy stiffness about it. That is all as may be; the fact is that *Portrait of Alice Murdoch, 1856*, offers up a milestone: it was the first proper picture of a small girl that Dodgson ever took. It initiated what would be a quarter-century quest to capture all the unmitigated charm and delight of the young girls who would befriend him and who he, in turn, would befriend.

He wrote the girl a brief stanza of thanks, and, carefully, in his best copperplate, inscribed it opposite her picture in the very first of his photo albums:

O child! O new born denison
Of life's great city! On thy head
The glory of the morn is shed
Like a celestial benison

There were to be many other Alice Murdochs in the years ahead, their names listed in his instantly recognizable hand, a nearly endless roll call of Victorian prepubescence: Charlotte, Rosellen, Rosamond, Adelaide, Lucy, Sarah, Eliza, Mary, Kathleen, Emily, and, nearly the most famous of all, the girl who was his chief model in his closing years of photography, Xie Kitchen.

His utter fascination with all of these girls, his need to picture them with or without clothing, his need to make them happy, to amuse them, to have them think of him as a friend and for him to feel free to do the same, his need to buy them dresses and stockings and bonnets and shoes, and on rare occasions to exhibit brief flashes of physical affection, reflect an aspect of Charles Dodgson's character that puzzles and intrigues to this day. Scores of books and essays have subsequently tried to probe the motives that led to his fondness for small children; they have enjoyed varying degrees of success. However, although Alice Murdoch can fairly be said to be the first young girl to be captured by Dodgson's camera, and perhaps the first to captivate him, it was to be another Alice altogether on whom the world's attention would eventually focus. This, of course, was Alice Pleasance Liddell, and she was, at the time, little more than four years old.

Dodgson, now gaining the necessary skills of his new pastime, was quite determined that he should meet her once again, that he should take her photograph in all manner of poses and costumes. He also resolved that he should take her and her sisters on journeys by boat or on foot across the countryside, and when settled down in the grass or in still waters beside the bank, entertain them.

Over the coming years he would develop his photographic skills still further, and he would consolidate his friendship with Alice Liddell to the point that he could photograph her in the garden of her college home, and then in time tell her the beginnings of a story that would eventually make both of them famous.

Chapter Six

A PORTRAIT MOST PERFECT
AND CHASTE

CHARLES DODGSON SOON BECAME A MASTER IN THE USE OF natural light. There was little choice: illumination in Victorian households was poor, guttering candles and gas lamps providing the only source (it would not be until the 1880s that electrical power began to offer a brighter alternative). Early photographic emulsions required lengthy exposure to light, and it was hardly surprising that more than a few photographers chose a little artificial help: Talbot, for instance, worked out a way of making flashes using the static electricity that was produced in Leyden jars, and these flashes enabled him to take some pictures in near darkness. And others went so dangerously far as to light magnesium ribbon or even thermite powder to produce brief bursts of intense light that would either help them expose in dim light, or else cut down the exposure time needed to photograph a subject.

But most of the early followers of the craft worked as best they could with what they had, and simply prayed hard for fine weather and long days. Oscar Rejlander, a Swedish-born portraitist who settled in London—and whose techniques and sensitivity Dodgson much admired—had a peculiar trick: he would place his very biddable cat where the sitter would eventually pose—and if by gazing into the cat's eyes it seemed to Rejlander there was enough light to give a good reflection, he would invite the sitter in. If the feline eyes were dulled, he would ask his subject to come back another day. He did this once with Dodgson himself. The Rejlander portrait of him remains one of the best known, adorning the jackets of scores of Dodgson books published around the world.

Rejlander himself had a changeling reputation. In his own early days—before he embarked on creating the formal portraits for which he would become so famous—he had a fascination with the erotic, and produced a series of *tableaux vivants* in which circus performers and young prostitutes were employed to pose, semi-clad or quite bare. But then Queen Victoria handed over ten guineas for a later Rejlander photograph, as a gift for Prince Albert. Suddenly legitimate, and with the gift of royal patronage, Rejlander was promptly endowed with a stature he enjoys to this day.

A few weeks after leaving Alice Murdoch behind in Putney, Dodgson took the train north to Yorkshire and, once settled in, began work on a series of photographs that display his fast-growing range of talents. His first work of note is a portrait he made of his father, Archdeacon Charles Dodgson, shortly after his arrival.

A considerate son, he was hesitant to put the elder Dodgson through the rigors of posing in low light; the Reverend Dodgson was fifty-six years old—old for a Victorian—and found having to sit without moving for so long discommoding at the very least. So, young Dodgson built a studio outdoors in the rectory garden, with a black velvet backdrop supported by stepladders, a carpet on the floor, and a heavy high-backed black chair dragged from the study. There is little in the resulting picture that suggests this was anywhere other than where the archdeacon was wont to compose his sermons.

The result is a triumph of composition and care. The Reverend Dodgson is shown sitting upright, his body turned to his right, his hands clasped together in his lap, his feet—in buckled shoes—stretched out before him. He is in his clerical black robes and collar. His face is turned towards the lens, a look of the faintest amusement, more evident in his twinkling eyes than in his slightly down-turned mouth. It is an expression that suggests the very opposite of Alice Murdoch's: this is a man fully engaged with the photographer, radiating tenderness and interest and assurance, precisely as a father might view his son—indulgently and tolerantly.

A short while later, Dodgson ventured to take his camera and associated bottles and tents inside the rectory, to risk the difficulties of working in much lower levels of light. He decided to make the best use possible of the enormous Georgian windows in the drawing room—having swept back the thick velvet curtains that would normally keep the rooms within private and warm—and assembled his remaining resident family there, reduced now to just three of his sisters. As he prepared his glass plates, he asked them to reflect particularly on the memory of their mother, who had died five years before, when first he had gone up to Oxford.

The resulting image, so different from the charmingly tender image of his father, is a study in grief and melancholy. It is presented in the impeccably apposite surroundings of a spare and under-furnished room, and is notable for the contrasting fields of light and shadow that perfectly match the mood. Two of the girls gaze absently into the distance; one is standing, the curve of her face echoed by that of a porcelain jug behind her. The other sits, and clearly moved a little, since her face is slightly blurred—though the blur works to the overall advantage of the picture, obscuring the details of her very evident expression of longing. The third girl—and here is the element that transforms this picture from mere silver-iodide recording into something approaching art—is entirely obscured by shadow, and one can spy only her outline, as if in a Victorian silhouette. Her skirts are visible, but not her face; it might just as easily be her late mother, with her daughters staring past her into the distance, wondering.

Dodgson had almost five months of indolence and delight that summer—Oxford terms were punctuated, as now, by extraordinarily periods of repose. But he worked hard at his new craft. By the time he was ready to go back to his top-floor rooms in Tom Quad he had already exposed and developed no fewer than eighty glass-plate negatives.

All are numbered, annotated, catalogued, and placed in albums. Most are now kept safe in vaults in Texas, and they provide a time-lapse image of Dodgson's life, a chart of his ever-increasing proficiency.

The places he went, lugging his Ottewill and his chemicals, the destinations later spelled out in that violet ink in that curious majuscule writing (but for some years not numbered—violet ink was not made until 1870, so he must have labeled his pictures a good dozen years after he began his work)—provide a list that might have a timetable for a Cook's tour of northern England:

Whitburn, Crosthwaite, Portinscale, the Lake District, Whitby, Alvaston.

The images that survive are almost all portraits—one or two are views (*Skiddaw, from south*), there are some buildings (*Alvaston House*), and some are of the anonymous (*Profile of Man Reading*). But most are of people; and many of these are children. Katherine Wilcox, pictured on Tyneside, was twelve; Charlotte Webster, photographed near Keswick, was nine; and when he came to Alvaston and happened upon Margaret Poole, a very distant and very pretty relative, he was twenty-four and she was just eight years old.

By the time he returned to Oxford that October it would be fair to say that however his artistic sensibilities may have been developing—or the degree to which, others will say, they were falling in with the temper of the times—he had made of himself a fully accomplished photographer: he was organized and fastidious and careful.

Many other young men of the day had taken up photography: to be seen carrying around a camera, or having the telltale stains of silver iodide on your hands or your clothing, was to make you out as excitingly *au courant*.

Moreover, photographs themselves had become objects of impassioned desire for those unable to afford the time or cost of indulging in the new art. Small albumen-print portraits of men, women, children, pets, and favorite places, printed on stiff cards, and known both because of the invention in France, and because of their similarity in size to the calling cards left by hopeful visitors, as *cartes-de-visites*, were manufactured and sold in prodigious numbers. Albums were made, enthusiasts known as *cardistes* indulged in an obsession known as *cardomania*, and there was trading, much as there was to be with cigarette cards and baseball cards in later years. The entire British royal family was depicted on one set of *cartes*—hastening their popularity, and prompting Dodgson, who had at first been somewhat disdainful of what he initially considered a vulgar hobby, to begin a collection himself.

By doing so, by amassing and comparing, he was able to gauge the aesthetic quality of the popular portraits and compare them with the images he was making. He came away reassured: what he was doing was honest and true, while the commercial images, despite their siren attraction, were meretricious at best. Except, of course, for those of the queen.

All too many of photography's early acolytes soon tired of the technical demands of their newfound calling. The batches of new photographic magazines that were being published in the late 1850s brimmed with advertised appeals from the frustrated and the despairing: the dropout rate was alarmingly high. But Dodgson, for one, never wavered. His first choice of camera was central: it was compact, it was light, it was versatile, and it could make images of different sizes, ranging from an entire 6 1/2 by 8 1/2 inches down to quarter-plate sizes of 3 1/4 by 4 1/4—this, it must be remembered, was before the invention of the enlarger (which, since solar-illuminated models were so unreliable, depended on the dissemination of electric power in the 1880s). He did in fact acquire during the coming months at least two other cameras, offering even greater flexibility; and in later years he was taking matters seriously enough to seek premises in the center of Oxford in which to build a semi-permanent darkroom—before the Christ Church authorities allowed him that aforementioned and unprecedented privilege of creating a darkroom and studio above his suite of rooms on Tom Quad.

But that was much later. For now he was simply an obsessive photographer, determined above all else to learn all that he could and not to be defeated by the difficulties involved. Of this the entire Senior Common Room at Christ Church knew; and so did the dean and Mrs. Liddell. Their friendly and extended cooperation was the key to what took place next.

Within days of his return south for the start of Michaelmas term, Dodgson was already using the Liddell's private garden at Christ Church for photographic sessions with other subjects. His catalogued photographs 148 (the eight-year-old Margaret Poole), 150 (her father), and 155 (their family house) were all taken in Derbyshire in early October 1856. In late October he was back in Oxford, where he took photograph 158, of Robert Godfrey-Faussett, his predecessor as a lecturer in mathematics and then the college steward. But crucially, the photograph is taken in the deanery garden. His blossoming friendship with the Liddells was sufficient for him to use this private and secluded oasis to practice his chosen art.

And so the Oxford pictures mount up—not all taken in the same garden, but most of them. There is a picture of a kitten, another of an old lady in a hairnet, and a carefully composed view—stunning as a piece of Oxford landscape photography— taken looking down from rooms in the Meadow Building, at the Broad Walk across Christ Church Meadow. But, of course, most are portraits of people, and many are children; most were taken in the Liddell gardens, and very many are of the Liddell children.

Harry, who Dodgson very much admired for his beauty on their first meeting, was illustrated first—and this time rather more successfully than when Southey persuaded him to come for a portrait in Dodgson's rooms, soon after the camera had been acquired.

One early afternoon he encountered Harry again, this time with Lorina, in the meadow, and persuaded the two of them to come to his rooms to see the photographs he had taken during the summer vacation. There was little doubt as to the allure of photographs; anyone invited in the mid-1850s to see examples of it would jump at the chance. It merely whetted the children's appetite for more, for opportunities to take part, to help Dodgson in any way they could.

In early November he met Miss Prickett, the governess whom he had so charmed when they first met the previous spring. She was walking Ina at the time, and Dodgson persuaded her to tell the dean that he would come on the next fine day to take a photograph of all the Liddell children, in the garden. His diary records his frustration—either the weather wouldn't cooperate, or the Liddells would go away, or there were moments of brief annoyance vaguely expressed, which caused him to draw back for fear of causing offense (in this case, in November 1856, he had taken one photograph of a professor of medicine in the dean's garden, but neglected to ask permission).

And then Mrs. Liddell had exploded in brief fury when he tried to take photographs of Harry and Lorina, alone. She would not allow him to take portraits unless all of them were in one large group. Once again he withdrew, chagrined. But it was only a few days later that the dean's exasperated wife relented, and she then had all of her children washed and dressed and their hair neatly brushed, to be marched en masse onto the lawn, and in front of the young man's tripod-mounted camera.

It was late fall 1856, and after a few clicks of lens caps and slide removal and development and fixing, all of the Liddell children were now recorded on one of his glass plates—a picture of historic significance that would be viewable now as image number 170, were it not that this single image has managed to get lost. One day it may turn up, but its existence is noted in Dodgson's diaries and catalogue notes, and its capture can fairly be said to mark the proper beginning of the full—if eventually rather troubled—relationship between Charles Dodgson and the Liddell family.

The catalogue of all three thousand of Dodgson's pictures—the final one of which we know is numbered 2700 and was taken in 1880, when he abandoned his hobby—lists 184 images as standing between that misplaced family picture taken in November 1856 and the capture of the best-known image that was taken of Alice on her own, eighteen months later. In other words, Dodgson would make on average ten images a month between his first professional encounter with the Liddell children and his most famous encounter with just one.

Each picture was still a careful elaboration, for this was half a century before the birth of the technical ability to take a "snapshot." (This was a word—first *snap-shot*, then *snapshot*, finally *snap*—which first appeared in the lexicon at exactly this time—the *Oxford English Dictionary* records the astronomer Sir John Herschel employing it in *Photography News* in 1860. But that doesn't mean the concept had become real: Herschel writes only to speculate on the possibility that one day one might make a *snap-shot* with a camera and a plate able to accommodate exposure as brief as a tenth of a second—and this at a time when forty-five-second exposures were still common. The word begins to turn up more often when such a possibility did become a reality, but that was thirty years later.)

Summertime was the most suitable for camera work: the days were long, the light was strong. The summer of 1857 was especially productive for Dodgson; not only did he engage in his customary portraiture, he also embarked on an extraordinary series of photographic investigations of animal skeletons, which were to be found in abundance in a museum of anatomical specimens in the college itself. (The collection was moved in its entirety from Christ Church to the Oxford Museum of Natural History in 1860. Many of Dodgson's subject-specimens can be seen there still, though they huddle in the shadow of the museum's most famous and iconic skeleton, that of the last dodo ever known. This was a skeleton with which Dodgson was very familiar; its later appearance in his writings, as a caricature of himself, is said to derive from his stuttering inability to say his own name: *Do-do-dodgson.*)

The skeleton pictures were all done at the request of the man under whose inspiration the university museum was founded, Regius Professor of Medicine Henry Acland, who was a student of Christ Church also and, as it happens, was the Liddell family doctor. Acland wanted a full record of exactly what was being passed from Christ Church to the university, and so Dodgson's pictures, his first true professional commission, are designed for accuracy rather than art. They were all taken in strong sunlight, and are crisp and beautiful and memorably fine. They begin with the remains of a brown kiwi, then move on to an anteater, a tuna, the head and shoulders of a cod (so described in his caption, though this was a jest derived from a colloquial saying of the time that a fool was *a person with a cod's head and shoulders*), a stupendous sunfish, and a group of students carefully examining the tiny skeleton of a sea creature.

They finish with a grand flourish: a *tableau semi-vivant* of the skeletons and skulls of humans and monkeys and, standing beside a human skeleton of exactly the same height and gazing in the same direction as the skeleton's head, his old friend Reginald Southey, very much live, clothed, and dignified. The progress of man, as it were, from right to left: the monkeys look to the left, implying a gaze into the backwardness from whence they came, while Southey and his bony doppelgänger look to the right, into the rising sun of the new dawn into which they are about to venture. It is an arresting image, at first somewhat ludicrous, but on close inspection powerfully symbolic and offering yet another insight into Dodgson's formidably figured mind.

He was able to conclude his association with the new museum with a spectacular coup in 1860. The staging there of the great and famous debate over Darwinism—*The Origin of Species* having been published the year before—brought to Oxford all the debate's principals, churchmen and scientists alike. The church essentially lost the argument, but Dodgson won the day, by arranging to photograph almost every distinguished figure who attended, doing so in a makeshift studio that he set up in—where else?—the Christ Church deanery garden.

But we are getting ahead of ourselves. The summer of 1860 may have placed Dodgson near the head of the league of English photographic portraitists of the time, enabling him to request and secure almost any subject he cared to picture—Lord Tennyson, Holman Hunt, the Prince of Denmark. He photographed his heroes, and the heroic style of his photography—with as props any number of velvet curtains, Grecian vases, floral bouquets, Corinthian columns—ennobled them still further. The summer of 1857, three years earlier, is more truly critical. For this is when he first started to take pictures of Alice Liddell on her own and to forge the friendship that lies at the core of his legacy.

The first picture of Alice alone was made on June 2, 1857, and it is numbered, without remark, simply as *No. 195: Liddell,*

Alice Pleasance, facing forward. At the time, she was five years and twenty-six days old. The final portrait of her alone, which Dodgson also took in Oxford—though not in the college, but in a studio he had set up for himself in rooms he had hired from an upholsterer named Richard Badcock just across St. Aldate's from the Christ Church main entrance—was made in 1870, when Alice was a little over eighteen years old, and about to be launched onto the London social scene.

A point is worth making here. Between those two photographic caryatids, the first and the last, the very visible bookends of a generally invisible and floating friendship, there are just nine other solo portraits of the girl—meaning that all the fuss and bother that surrounds the relationship between Charles Dodgson and Alice Liddell has a mere eleven images to show for it. If the photographs in which Alice is depicted with her sisters or brothers are added, the number climbs by a further seven. In total, then, just eighteen photographs exist that show Alice as she was selected, interpreted, and recorded by Dodgson—many fewer pictures than he took of some of his later special child-friends—and yet they possess a significance today quite out of proportion to the number of exposures.

The first has a fine simplicity about it, both in its reproduction and its content. It is cut into an oval, almost four inches tall and three inches wide—Dodgson was meticulous in the shaping of his pictures, and one can see fine pencil tracings on the back of some images, marking where his razor should travel, or where the final picture should be matched against a template. In it Alice is seen sitting to the left of the center line, and on a severely straight chair that is itself artfully placed slightly off to the right of the center line. We are told that the picture was taken in the garden, but there is a backdrop of cotton muslin that obscures any suggestion of foliage, and only the bright illumination suggests that the sun was shining, as well it might have been on the early June day of the session.

The girl is dressed in what was probably a white or pink dress, lightly patterned with flowers, and with ruffled sleeves and shawl collar. Her hair, brushed from a center parting, falls to just a little below her ears. Her hands are clasped together, in her lap. She is looking directly into the lens, her chubby-cheeked face essentially expressionless, though perhaps with a look of slight impatience, as if she longed to get back to playing.

The last, taken twelve years later, in the rooms that Dodgson had rented from Richard Badcock, seems almost to be of an entirely different person. Alice's arrival at the studio came as a great surprise to Dodgson. He had been working on a series of portraits of Lord Salisbury (and his twelve-year-old daughter, Maud), and had had little contact with the Liddells at all for the previous five years; certainly there had been no photography of any of the family for the previous decade. Then, all of a sudden and quite without warning, Mrs. Liddell arrived at the studio with Lorina and Alice in tow. Ina was now twenty-one years old; Alice, three years younger than her sister, was also no longer a child but very much a young lady in appearance and behavior.

Dodgson, well schooled in the most elaborate of courtesies, naturally exulted in the arrival of the girls, who he still called his "favourites," as they undoubtedly still were. But he was probably disappointed by Alice's appearance—rather more so, perhaps, than he had been when they had met five years before. "She seems changed a great deal," he wrote of that meeting, "and hardly for the better, probably going through the usual awkward stage of transition."

He did not care for the physical trials of adolescence; nor—according to the myth of Lewis Carroll, a myth lately exploded by the British author Karoline Leach, who asserted in 1999, after much study, that he had as great a fondness for grown women as for children—did he always unreservedly admire the arrival of adulthood, having, according to this myth, so treasured the nymph and nymphet that Alice had once so eternally seemed to be. But even Charles Dodgson could not argue with the progress of biology, and so he sat the girls down for their pictures—Lorina first, and then Alice.

Of the two images, Alice's is by far the more powerful and haunting. She is sitting this time not in an austere nursery chair but in a high leather-backed chair with padded arms, a piece of hastily chosen furniture much more suitable for a clubbable man, a parliamentary Lord Salisbury or a poetic Lord Tennyson. Alice looks too small for the chair, even now; she is resting neither of her arms on the chair, but keeps them together and in her lap, using the chair as a tiny sanctuary. Her dress is necessarily much more elaborate and very much of the period: silk shantung in a dark pastel, with a bodice, a boutonnière, and a cotton high-necked blouse, finished with a small locket around her neck. She has no other jewelry. Her hair is long, and worn up well off her neck, and she has a colored ribbon.

She is facing to her right—forward to her future, if we assume the same convention here as the photographer had adopted in the Southey-and-skeleton pictures. And yet her face wears a tragic look of such ineluctable sadness that the viewer has to wonder: *What on earth is wrong?* Does life's prospect hold no comfort or pleasant mystery? Is it really all a torment? Or is it all a joke, a charade? Did perhaps the now thirty-eight-year-old Reverend

Dodgson, a man who, after all, would have to abandon his studentship at the college, and thus his entire academic career, if ever he dared to seek your hand, did he ask you to act out an artificial misery, to suggest to the world an image of hopelessness—merely to underline for all to see his own pain at losing you to the great outside?

Although this image of Alice Liddell is much less well known than the image that is the central subject of this account, I find it the most puzzlingly enigmatic, the most arresting of all. Her expression is maddeningly odd—especially since we know well the life of jollity and glamour upon which she was about to embark, and which included her supposedly enjoying an affair, right off the bat, with no less a personage than Leopold, Duke of Albany—a Christ Church undergraduate who also happened to be one of Queen Victoria's children. To become involved with a royal might be a daunting prospect, to be sure—but hardly one to engender such an expression of unrestrained woe.

Between these two pictures—between that first which captured the bland innocence of the six-year-old child and the second, which conveys the seemingly deep melancholy of the young woman—stands the famous one, taken when Alice was but six years old and yet seemed to be already well aware of her powers.

Volumes have been written about the friendship between Charles Dodgson and the Liddell household. Studies of its complexities have tended to concentrate on just seven of the deanery residents: Henry Liddell himself; his wife, Lorina, younger by fifteen years; the oldest boy, Harry; the three sisters, Ina, Alice, and Edith; and Mary Prickett, the governess. (With Lorina said, somewhat unkindly, to be a "fertile" woman, six other children were to be born to the dean: James, who died of scarlet fever when he was three; Rhoda, who died in 1949; Albert, who was born in 1863 but died in infancy; Violet, who lived until 1927; Frederick— later Sir Frederick Liddell—who died in 1950; and Lionel, who was born in 1868 and died in 1942. None of these offspring merit more than an occasional passing note in Dodgson's writings. Nor does the academy devote much time to them: the friendships of the seven principals provide more than enough grist for a thousand mills.)

With Henry Liddell, Dodgson appears to have had, as we've seen, an affable relationship, entirely in line with that of senior and junior members of the same privileged group of men. Certainly, it was good enough for the dean at one stage to stop pressing the younger man to take Holy Orders, as his studentship required him to do, and to ignore the college statutes by permitting him to remain secure in his position and his rooms even though he was breaking the rules.

Mrs. Liddell's position is rather more complex. She was a headstrong woman, said by her detractors to have a "fiery" temper that suggested to these same critics a Spanish ancestry, to go with her dark hair and somewhat sallow complexion (she was entirely British, and came from what some snobbish observers remarked was a less-than-impeccably well-born family in Lowestoft). So it is perhaps unsurprising that there were tiffs and fallings-out with the constant visitor who had almost set up shop in the deanery, going so far as to leave chemicals and equipment there, as though it were his personal photographic supply room.

Small wonder Mrs. Liddell was on occasion exasperated with Dodgson. But the widely held notion that theirs was a relationship marked by hostility and suspicion—as in a *keep away from my children* kind of suspicion, a suspicion twinned with the mythic view of him as having unnatural urges towards his "child-friends," and most especially those in her own family—seems entirely wrong.

Mrs. Liddell, pinioned as she was in a society of much older men whose discussions and interests were almost entirely serious and most often declared with the most studious solemnity, was achingly bored at times; to have just a few hundred feet away through the cloisters the company of a young man with manners and charm and a compellingly strange imagination, and who clearly adored her children, who in turn adored him—logic alone suggests that the two of them ought to have gotten along famously.

And there is evidence, too: letters of invitation, records of visits that she made to his rooms on Staircase 7, diary notes of enthusiasm and pleasure, all testimony to the simple fact that the two of them, so similar in age (she was a mere six years older than Dodgson), so joined in their vivacity of mind, their sense of fun, their common interests, liked each other's company.

Then there were the four children. The oldest, Harry, had been adored by Dodgson since they first met in 1856, for both his boyish beauty and high spirits. The feeling was evidently mutual. As an eight-year-old, the child followed Dodgson like a puppy, always amazed, always delighted. There was an element of hero worship: "You've got your white gown on and *you read in church!*" he exclaimed one day astonished.

And little wonder Harry thought of Dodgson as hero. Not only was he filled with ideas and inventions and games—not only was he wildly interesting, in the way father Liddell was evidently not—but he liked the children, too, paid attention to them. Dodgson also liked helping Harry in practical ways, showing him clever ways to do his sums, something that all rambunctious little boys find admirable.

It was much the same with Lorina—Ina—though here there was something more intimate in the friendship, something less tangible, more secret. During what Dodgson much later called "that foolish time that seemed as if it would last forever"— by which he meant the decade from 1856 to 1866, from the time he met the Liddells to the moment when his book became a sensation—he and Lorina became the very closest of friends.

The record shows him mentioning her, and doing so invariably most affectionately, many more times than the other sisters. This is *the fourteenth time* I have been with her to the river, he writes at one point, and one can almost hear in those words the wistful counting of all the previous excursions, and the fevered hope that there might be a fifteenth, and more.

There was some later suspicion voiced, though only when Ina was more grown up—taller and with a fair figure—that Dodgson might have considered her a potential spouse. There is much discussion over a summary of those pages razored from one of his diaries.

Dodgson kept meticulous diaries for every year of his life from 1853 onward. But four of them—including two that cover five and a half years of that first decade, a period central to "that foolish time"—have gone missing; and several other pages have been carefully removed, presumably by, or at the request of, Stuart Collingwood, the nephew who became Dodgson's first official biographer. The summary of some of these missing pages, crucial to the understanding of Dodgson during what most who are fascinated by him regard as the most intriguing period of his life, was found by chance, in 1996, by Karoline Leach. The summary, which appears to have been written by Dodgson's niece Violet, says only that "he is also supposed by some to be courting Ina." And from that has come a flurry of suggestions that have kept students of Carrolliana busy, if not necessarily amply fed, for many years since.

There is, however, one alternative assertion about Dodgson in that same summary: the charge, made apparently without rancor by Mrs. Liddell herself, "that he is supposed to be using the children as a means of paying court to the governess." This brings briefly to the fore one other member of the Liddell household—the governess Mary Prickett, who was not a comely woman by any means, and was less well educated than others in the deanery. In such diaries as survive Dodgson reacts with incredulity that anyone should think him as tipping his hat to Miss Prickett. In any case, she had her own eye on a gentleman who went on to become landlord of the Mitre Hotel. She eventually married him and settled into a life of blameless urban domesticity, well beyond the rarified atmosphere of the Christ Church deanery.

Of Edith Liddell, the youngest of the three sisters at the time of his arrival, there is little to suggest any more than dutiful affection on Dodgson's part. She is always there—accompanying her brother and two sisters on expeditions, boating journeys, and picnics; and she is photographed, but only three times alone, twice lying on a sofa, once in high summer, "with foxgloves." Perhaps it was because she was not quite so pretty—she was a redhead, with a Pre-Raphaelite look that Dodgson might have found less attractive than the sultry pout of Ina or the darkly Iberian look of the others.

And the catalogue of the Liddell portraits certainly illustrates the degree of preference—favoritism, maybe?—in which Dodgson indulged. For in the albums of photographs, in Princeton, Oxford, Austin (Texas), and New York, it is Edith just occasionally,

Lorina a good deal, Harry many times in the early days—and then all of a sudden just three girls, either all together, or then two of them, Lorina and Alice, Edith and Alice, Lorina, Edith, and Alice, and then just Alice.

Alice Pleasance Liddell was peculiarly and particularly special to Charles Dodgson and, in time, to all of us. And it shows, in the pictures. As we've seen, there were to be just eleven of them. The picture that above all others is the most admired, contentious, and unforgettable is the fourth in the series.

The first one is that one taken at the beginning of June 1857—the one that has her looking directly at the camera; in the second, she is facing to the left. In the third, Dodgson had an idea born of his aforementioned fascination with the poetry of Tennyson (who he would photograph many times over during his career, starting in the Lake District just six months later, during his coming long vacation from Oxford). But, as we've seen, it was "The Beggar Maid," written in 1833 but published in 1844, about the love of a king for a servant-girl, that had set Victorian hearts to stirring; and on that particular June afternoon, it seemed right that with Alice—five-year-old Alice—being as untouchable and unavailable a subject of veneration for Dodgson as Penelophon had been for Cophetua—she should be the subject of a suitably allegorical photograph, a picture that, unlike the kind of portraits that had dominated his work thus far, could be allowed *to tell a story*.

And so, afire with this idea, Dodgson had her go back and up to her bedroom in the deanery, there to be dressed by her mother and by Miss Prickett in as shabby an outfit as could be found, and then return to be photographed. Depicted as a flower-girl in the *Pygmalion* myth, she is barefoot, her white rags standing out sharply against the backcloth background of his improved garden set. She has her hand cupped, waiting for a coin. She is looking upward, pleadingly, as though at a benefactor much taller than she is, hoping that he will not pass ungenerously by.

It is a cleverly composed photograph, and it was a modest success, but modest only. It remains today, rarely seen, in the library at Christ Church. The family album that holds it had been bought at auction by an American collector and loaned back to the college, of which he was an alumnus. Yet it is of no mean historical significance, for it left an idea lingering in Dodgson's head; and a year later, after ranging around the country taking photographs of everything and everyone he found fascinating, from Lord Tennyson and his family down to "Tim, the Dodgson family doll," he was back in Oxford, and ready to put his plan into execution.

He would, according to the plan, have Alice act out a story. He set up his camera in the deanery garden once more, though this time he left his backcloth behind. And he summoned the girls, Alice first. And this time, he told her, she should bring with her some changes of costume.

He would have her act out for his camera a tale in two parts— or maybe three. The absence of Dodgson's diaries for these years leaves some room for ambiguity and speculation. There happens to be a third photograph, dated and located similarly, "summer 1858, Deanery Garden," but it does not have the appearance of the third item in a triptych. In this particular image, Alice, dressed smartly and sitting in a hard chair, looks to the right; the garden wall is vaguely visible, out of focus, behind her. And her hair seems just a little shorter than in the two more famous images, further hinting that it is not part of a series of three. The suspicion has to be that it was taken a day or so earlier, perhaps as preparation for the allegorical pair.

Let us imagine, then, that Dodgson required Alice to come down from the deanery with just two outfits. What he had in mind was a very brief moral tale, a picture-driven story of a smart little girl brought low by tragedy or ill fortune, then transformed into a girl who, cunning beyond the imagination of her elders and her peers, convincingly acts the impoverished seducer, and assumes an expression and a demeanor so very different from that she had offered to her world.

In the first picture Alice is a well-dressed six-year-old girl, ready for a garden party or for afternoon tea. She is neat and tidy and deferential and well-mannered—though evidently a child born of frugal parents, for the dress she is wearing is quite clearly the same as that in which she was photographed the year before, just after her fifth birthday.

In that earlier image she was sitting down, her dress bunched up a little around her chest and looking tented, as though it might have been a little large for her. But this following summer, standing in the flowerbed, her form now a little taller and her figure somewhat more robust, she fills the dress and looks entirely *right* in it, as though it might have been made for her (as perhaps it was, with Miss Prickett's skills as a seamstress).

The picture duly taken, Dodgson then asks her to run back to her mother. He scurries back inside his tent, and, in near-total darkness, smoothes a new smear of collodion paste onto a second glass plate. Next, and with now well-practiced fingers, he slides and clamps this plate into place in the back of the Ottewill camera, checks that the clasps and buckles are tightly shut and that all is ready for the next picture, then reemerges into the afternoon sunshine. He fixes the camera once more on top of the tripod and adjusts it to point in the direction of the garden wall, at the very place where Alice had been standing so prettily a moment before.

And then back through the old deanery doorway comes Alice for this second time, clad on this occasion in rags and with her feet quite bare. Concerned lest she hurt herself on the stones, he demands of the gardener a carpet from the greenhouse, and then places the shabby piece of colored sisal on the ground, just in front of the corner shrubbery that was trampled during the last session. He tells Alice to step back to the wall, to lean against it, to place her left foot on the wooden garden border and her right on the carpet. He arranges the nasturtiums around her bare feet, the clematis by her right side. He arranges the rags around her knees. He places her arms *just so*—her left bent and with her fist pinioned against her waist, her right hand cupped in supplication.

Is Mrs. Liddell watching? Is Lorina in the garden? And Edith? (Both would have been close, since they were having their own pictures taken later that same afternoon.) Would anyone care that Dodgson then reached behind the little girl's hair and adjusted the off-white garment about her shoulders, such that it fell slightly from her left and exposed only just entirely her left nipple? Is it prurient or prudent to notice such a thing?

Certainly, Dodgson's interest in small girls—he photographed scores of them, and a significant number of them nude (though only four of these images remain, each now hand-colored and thus rendered inoffensively artistic)—fascinates many in today's more exposed world. Many have weighed in on Dodgson's supposed sexual predilections. Victorian attitudes toward young children held that they were the literal embodiment of innocent beauty, an innocence to be preserved and revered. All surviving evidence suggests that Dodgson's attitude was no different and that his interest in the Liddell girls during their prepubescent years was unremarkable, in every sense of the word.

For the next few seconds of that summer afternoon his particular fascination is a matter of only immediate consequence. There was a job that needed to be done. Technique was by far the most important thing. So Dodgson stands back, tells Alice to take a deep breath and relax and stare with dreamy intensity into the camera's single brass-bound Ross lens, and to think of something vague and pleasant and good, and then hold the look, without a smile or a blink of an eye.

And so, with all the practiced ease that she has displayed for her previous three solo pictures, she does as she is told. She stands as directed, the talking around her stills, all eyes are fixed on this little girl, and the garden falls quiet.

From beneath his black velvet shroud, Dodgson then raises his hand to signal that the lens is open. He counts to five, to ten, to twelve—no one speaks, no one moves. It is hot, airless, silent. And then finally, just when the tension seems fit to crack, he drops his hand. It is all over. The plate was exposed. The picture *was*.

Alice was dismissed. She ran off to join her sister and her mother and to change out of her ragged shift. Dodgson, ducking back into his artificially dark world, removed the plate into storage, and listed it to be taken for development and printing.

On seven further occasions Dodgson was able to take images of the girl alone, but he already had the image that he wanted. Now matters that involved him and this one young girl would take a different turn.

For on a blazing summer's afternoon four years after this photograph was taken, Alice Pleasance Liddell, who by then was ten years old, would ask her friend Charles Dodgson a single simple question.

———

It was July 4, 1862, and he was taking her and the other Liddell girls, as he had done many times before, on a picnic expedition along the river, to Godstow. While he was rowing in the bow, his friend Robinson Duckworth—a giant of a man from Trinity College, a man with a fine baritone voice, who later became chaplain to the queen—was rowing stroke, and the three children, whom he nicknamed Prima, Secunda, and Tertia—were fooling about in the well of the craft, trailing their hands in the water, eating strawberries and chicken, and drinking ginger beer.

They were also listening with rapt intent to a story that Charles was telling them about a little girl who had fallen down a rabbit-hole and into a curious new world. Duckworth, at first only half-listening, soon became quite astonished by the strange intricacies of the yarn. Was this an *extempore* tale, he asked Charles at one point, as he paused his rowing. *Oh yes, I am just making it up as I go along*, his friend replied.

The story went on, with short breaks, while they stopped under the weeping willow trees at Godstow, as they gazed and ate their sandwiches and drank their pop, and when Charles snoozed or pretended to, as a tease, for all of the rest of that famous "golden afternoon." And then they turned for home. The summer sun started to slant down over the elms and the oaks and the riverbank poplars, and afternoon came to its inevitable end and the boat splashed gently back downstream and under the cool shadows of Folly Bridge back into Oxford; and after the boatman had tied up the craft and the two men and the three little girls walked happily back up the Broad Walk through the meadow to the college and to the deanery door, so Alice asked the fateful question. Would Mr. Dodgson kindly one day write down this quite extraordinary story and in due course present it to her as a gift?

He replied that he would try to do so, and bade the children good night. According to Duckworth, he was good to his word: he spent most of that very night in his rooms on Tom Quad writing down in a green-covered manuscript book all that he could remember, and more that he could now create, of the story of *Alice's Adventures Underground*. Page after page he covered with his neat, blocky writing, and he made small sketches in the margins and within the text, and he played with the text, making the very words twist and turn on the page, just for fun.

This story was never going to go away, never evaporate as so many of his earlier picnic tales had, into the summer air. Alice began to pester him for it. It must have been much better than usual, she later recalled, because she just wouldn't let go of it. She kept on asking him, day after day—*where is my story? you promised, can I see it? how much have you written?* Yes, he insisted in reply, he was a man of his word. He would indeed give the story to her, one day.

It took him a while to fulfill his promise. There was much else to do—his teaching, his college duties—and there was a sudden but temporary cooling in his friendship with the Liddell family, a break that has never been fully or properly explained, and that, in truth, never was fully and properly healed. But then, at the end of November 1864, a year and a half after he had first told her the tale, Dodgson presented to Alice as a Christmas gift the small green book of *Alice's Adventures Underground*, with its neatly written 15,500 words and its pretty illustrations.

At the very end of the story, he had drawn a small sketch of his girl, but evidently didn't care for it—for beside it he had placed an oval cut-out of a portrait he had taken of her in 1860.

The following year the book was published, by Macmillan. By then it had been expanded, almost doubled in length, to 27,500 words. John Tenniel, known for his illustrations in *Punch*, had provided forty-two drawings. The book was given a new title: *Alice's Adventures in Wonderland*. Its author was credited as being Lewis Carroll.

It sold sensationally from the moment it first appeared in London's bookshops. It has been translated into more than 125 languages, 100 editions have been created, and from the work innumerable plays and puppet shows and ballets and masques and films—including, inevitably, a porno version—have been rendered. And the book, one of the most popular in almost every language in which it has been published, has never been out of print.

Chapter Seven

AND THEN THE GIRL BECAME A LADY

IN THE MIDDLE OF THE SPRING OF 1932, MRS. ALICE HARGREAVES, an eighty-year-old widow living quietly in a large house in the New Forest of southern England, arrived in New York aboard the ocean liner *Berengaria*, to be besieged by photographers and mobbed by the press. She had already expressed her apprehension. "Alice of Wonderland Fears Our Reporters" ran the headline in the *New York Times* on April 19. She had already issued a public apology to the tens of thousands of American children who had written to her begging that she sign their books, explaining that she was eighty, tired easily, and could not possibly accede to their demands—yet did not want to appear standoffish or unkind.

A few days before leaving for New York, she had signed one copy, for the then six-year-old princess Elizabeth, the girl who would one day be queen: that one copy is one of a very few ever autographed by the woman who had won fame as "the original Alice," and who signed the flyleaf using those very words.

Alice had seen little of Charles Dodgson in the years that followed the cooling of relations between him and her family in the late 1860s. She had been fond of him, without a doubt; she had loved posing for his camera; she had been incontinently proud of the role she had played in the making of his book. But the rift—caused precisely by what still no one knows, though that recently discovered summary of some missing diary pages, as we've seen, hinted that it might have been because Dodgson was thought to have designs on Ina, Alice's older sister—had effects that echoed down the years. Alice did not acknowledge receiving her first edition of the book. He did not attend her eventual wedding in Westminster Abbey. She did not acknowledge the wedding gift he sent, or invite him to be sponsor to her children. His relationship with her parents had become distant, civil, rather cold.

Mrs. Liddell had always wanted the very best of husbands for her daughters. Lorina did well enough, marrying a man named W. B. Skene, a fellow of All Souls and a landowner of substance. Once Alice was old enough to be interested in the opposite sex, she became involved with Queen Victoria's youngest son, Prince Leopold, who had come up to study at Christ Church.

She had by this time grown into a classic beauty. The celebrated portraitist Julia Margaret Cameron photographed Alice, twice, when she was twenty. Both pictures were deliberately mirror images of those taken so many years before by Dodgson—the supplicant's cupped hand is the left one rather than the right, for example—and they show what he little saw, or maybe never wished to see: her physical attributes and frankly adult expression, reasons for men to bestow the kind of attention upon her in ways that he never did, or could.

The love affair with Leopold was very much of this kind, intense on both sides, and it pleased the snobbish Mrs. Liddell mightily. Yet it ended swiftly; once matters became serious a somewhat horrified Victoria whisked her boy away to marry into the much more suitable legion of German royalty.

Alice married a commoner in 1880, another wealthy Christ Church undergraduate and onetime student of Dodgson. He was Reginald Hargreaves, the son of the owner of a Lancashire calico mill. Hargreaves was a stylish, sporting, clever, and moneyed man with estates in both the north of England and in Hampshire, where he would in time inherit an elegant Georgian mansion known as Cufnells, near the New Forest town of Lyndhurst. After the wedding at Westminster Abbey, the couple moved into this vast house, and Alice—with the unacknowledged gift from Dodgson, a watercolor of Tom Quad, hanging above the drawing-room fireplace—lived there for the remainder of her long life.

Alice had three children, all boys. Alan was born first; Leopold second—the prince after whom the boy was named becoming godparent (and naming his own daughter Alice); and then a third son, whom she named Caryl. This last, a version of the first name of the author of *Alice's Adventures*, was her only public acknowledgment of her connection. Many were the occasions on which she could have offered a gesture; there were to be none.

She was glad, however, to receive a letter from him in 1892, telling of the success of the great book, which by that time had sold more than 120,000 copies, and she wrote a courteous but distant letter back. But when Dodgson died in 1898, and in a house in Surrey that stood not more than a day's journey from her

Hampshire estate, she did not publicly acknowledge the fact, nor did she attend the funeral. Neither did any other of the Liddell family. Just four days later, Henry Liddell himself died, a coincidence lost on few.

Alice's later years were suffused with a terrible sadness. Her life seemed initially as grand as her mother might have wished, with balls and soirees and all the trappings of gentrified society. But there was a lack to it, which all who knew her readily noticed. "However much she laughed and sang," wrote her biographer, "however much she indulged that insatiable curiosity, the sadness was somehow always there."

She missed something, and we all may like to imagine precisely what that something was: long-ago golden Oxford summer afternoons, that time of delicious foolishness, when Charles Dodgson would come a-calling and would take the photographs, and organize the picnics and the expeditions, and would tell the girls— and to her most devotedly—the most fantastic stories. A glittering society life and a thousand Hampshire balls could somehow never quite compete.

Come the Great War, and it all began to crumble anyway. Alan and Leopold were both killed at the front. Reginald Hargreaves, plagued by financial troubles, died in 1926, leaving Cufnells to Caryl, but without sufficient funds to enable him to maintain it and burdened with ruinous death duties. Caryl remained in London, an indolent wastrel and a spendthrift.

Alice stayed at Cufnells. To help pay the taxes she was compelled to sell all the memorabilia that connected her with Lewis Carroll. She sold, in particular, and by way of the Sotheby's auction house, the green manuscript book with Carroll's handwritten account of *Alice's Adventures Underground*. It fetched 15,400 pounds sterling—a huge sum in those days, more than enough to pay the taxes. But Caryl invested it imprudently, or worse, and before long it was all gone, too.

The manuscript was purchased first by an American, and then disappeared to the United States for a short while. After the end of the Second World War it was purchased by a group of Anglophilic book lovers in New York who sent it back to England "as an expression of thanks to a noble people who held Hitler at bay for a long period single-handed." It was hand-carried on the *Queen Elizabeth* by the librarian of Congress, kept under his pillow; in London it was formally accepted on behalf of the British people by the Archbishop of Canterbury. A "pure act of generosity," he called it. The book is still on display at the British Library, a favorite of all who visit.

As we've seen, Alice herself came to America in 1932 to help celebrate the centenary of Charles Dodgson's birth—her last formal acknowledgment of her connection to the story, and one that for many years she had done so little to advertise.

Columbia University put her up at the Waldorf-Astoria and awarded her an honorary doctorate of letters. Crowds greeted her, yelling, "Hey, Alice!" Police had to escort her everywhere. The radio broadcast an interview in which she suggested that her visit to America and New York City was so exciting that the experience, as she put it, took her "back to Wonderland." Few entirely believed it then. None do now.

Photographs taken by the New York press show a bewildered old lady, wrinkled and gray and evidently quite weary of having to play the part of that little golden girl of seventy years before. The golden afternoon that had made her so famous seemed so distant, fading away into memory.

In New York, the woman who inspired it all was pictured cruelly, and was but two years away from her own lonely death. Her face is quite unrecognizable, bearing no trace at all of that fixed and haunting gaze of 1858, no hint of the impish smile of knowingness that once played across her lips.

As one looks at that earlier picture today, and then is forced to turn away, or to turn the page, and then tries to remember it, like all photographs good or bad, its components start slowly to vanish.

First the surrounds begin to go—the borders and the frame and the quality of the light. Next the dark Oxford limestone walls behind the young girl start to fade, the clematis and the nasturtiums of the deanery gardens begin to vanish. Next the little girl's bare feet and her arms and the cupped hand and the bare chest and the shoulder all go. And before long we are left with the mouth and the tiny nose and the eyes, those magical, all-seeing eyes that Charles Dodgson managed to catch on that collodion-covered glass plate.

And then the eyes fade away, too, back into the camera-vault of the observer's mind. And like the smile of the Cheshire Cat, soon there is nothing left at all—merely the memory of the image, suspended weightless in the mind, playing tricks on it, such as only the very finest of photographs manage to do. The image of Alice Liddell, unforgettably young, unforgettably beautiful, once captured on the glass plate, then printed on the page, then pasted into an album bought, sold, collected, and finally consigned to the secure and deep darkness of Firestone Library, forever conjuring a wonderland of its very own.

End

SIMON WINCHESTER

ACKNOWLEDGMENTS

I AM MOST GRATEFUL TO CYBELE TOM FOR FIRST SUGGESTING the idea of writing the photographic backstory of the *Alice in Wonderland* saga. When she then left the press to pursue an entirely new and different career as a book conservator, she handed back this project to Timothy Bent, the Oxford University Press editor who is ultimately responsible for this photography series. Tim then performed on my words an edit of great skill and elegance, delicately turning what was at first a mere untidy assemblage into something that was both more streamlined and yet entirely appropriate to the era that the words seek to describe. Down in North Carolina, Christine Dahlin next applied her own similarly finely honed set of production editing skills to make the pages gleam: for Christine her work on this small book—as well as these modest thanks—must perforce serve as valedictory, since she has also left the press. She will be much missed, not least by the authors with whom she worked so conscientiously.

The doyen of Dodgson scholars, known round the world for his meticulous scholarship, is Edward Wakeling, whose cottage in Herefordshire has become a shrine to the scrupulously accurate remembrance of all things Alice and all things Carroll. He is pestered for help relentlessly, and it was generous of him to devote such time and thought as he did to this small volume: I am most grateful for his courtesy and remain awed by his knowledge.

The famous picture that lies at the heart of this book has for the past decade been locked inside a basement vault at Princeton University's Firestone Library, some well-cemented feet below the Parrish Library in which it was initially shelved. Though Steve Ferguson, the Curator of Rare Books, was more than happy to show me around the Parrish collection itself, his colleague Don Skemer, an authority on medieval textual amulets and the current Curator of Manuscripts, does not wish the Alice picture itself to be seen, ever. This, he explained, is the sole restriction applied to the Parrish material—and after some courteous chafing, I felt compelled to abide by his ruling. After all, he argued, the digital reproductions of the image offered in recompense were pixel-for-pixel identical, and there was thus no need to expose the original print to the destructive rigors of wind and sun.

His was a persuasive argument, for which I thank him; and it also seemed to offer me an appropriately Carrollian irony—in that it obliged me to write a book about a photograph that remains for me entirely unseen. Just like the Cheshire Cat, it is a picture that steadily faded into memory, leaving behind just Alice Liddell's enigmatic knowing smile, a fuzz of muddled sepia, and then nothing.

SUGGESTIONS FOR FURTHER READING

THE BIBLICAL AUTHORITY IN WHAT IS A VERY CROWDED FIELD IS *Lewis Carroll, Photographer*, by Roger Taylor and Edward Wakeling (Princeton University Press, 2002). Among other things it provides a register of what are believed to be all of Charles Dodgson's pictures, from his first simple portraits of 1856 to the more elaborated images with which he concluded his pastime twenty-four years later. As a supplement, I found very useful Robert Taylor's *Lewis Carroll at Texas* (Nos. 32/33 of the *Library Chronicle of the University of Texas at Austin*), which lists and illustrates many other works available for viewing in the legendary Harry Ransom Center.

Although Karoline Leach staggered the Carrollian world with her *In the Shadow of the Dreamchild* (Peter Owen, 1999 and 2009), her fascinating revelations and suggestions scarcely touched on Dodgson's work as a photographer, *sensu stricto*, other than by providing yet more illumination. And that is certainly true also of another recent work, Jenny Woolf's *The Mystery of Lewis Carroll* (Haus, 2010), which adds but the finest layer of new sediment to the story's steadily accumulating stratigraphy (including solemn speculation on whether his neurological health would have allowed him to get a driving license). It is testament to the enduringly enigmatic nature of the two *Alice* books that so much precious and quasi-academic scholarship now enfolds their study, with the years bringing groanings of new works—perhaps this one included, of course—that each adds but minutely to the patina of knowledge.

Yet despite all the fuss and pother over what has come to be known as the Carroll Myth—the customary view of the sexually unsophisticated and socially awkward Charles Dodgson, a view of which Ms. Leach is a most prominent challenger—none of these works have really managed yet to displace from his pedestal the confessedly traditionalist Morton Cohen (*Lewis Carroll: A Biography*; Macmillan, 1995).

Though speculation will doubtless continue for years as to whether Charles Dodgson was inclined this way or that, and whether he was bad, mad, sad, or none of the above, it seems doubtful that anyone will manage seriously to vitiate the authority of Professor Cohen, and for a long while to come. I happily used his book as *vade mecum*, and I suggest to anyone whose appreciation for Dodgson's remarkable skill as a photographer whets the appetite for a greater knowledge of Dodgson as man, writer, and creator of one of literature's most charming and complex invented creatures, that they crack open Mr. Cohen's lengthy book, and dive deep.

INDEX

H

Hargreaves, Alan, 93, 94
Hargreaves, Alice, 91–96.
    See also Liddell, Alice
    Pleasance
Hargreaves, Caryl, 93, 94, 95
Hargreaves, Leopold, 93, 94
Hargreaves, Reginald, 93, 94
heroic style of Dodgson's
    photography, 73
Herschel, Sir John, 71
Hume, Caroline, 58

I

insanity, 35–36

J

*Journal of the Photographic
    Society*, 48–49
Jowett, Benjamin, 22–23

K

Kitchen, Xie, 60

L

"The Lady of the Ladle"
    (Dodgson), 27

Leach, Karoline, 76, 80
lecturing career of Dodgson,
    32
Leopold, Prince, Duke of
    Albany, 77, 92, 93
Liddell, Albert, 78
Liddell, Alice Pleasance
    adult life of, 91–96
    arrival at Christ Church, 32
    beggar-girl image of, 5–8,
        84–86, 96, 98
    death of, 96
    and favoritism of Dodgson,
        57, 82
    first meeting with Dodgson,
        33, 34
    and picnic expedition, 87–88
    portraits of, 7, 73–77,
        82–84, 89, 92–93
    relationship of Dodgson
        with, 57, 60–61
    and story promised by
        Dodgson, 88–89
    trip to United States, 91,
        95–96
Liddell, Arthur, 31–32
Liddell, Edith
    arrival at Christ Church, 32
    and beggar-girl image of
        Alice, 85

lighting in early photography,
63, 71–72
London photography
exhibitions, 51

M

Macmillan, 89
magazines, photographic, 68
maternal love, 20
Mayor, Robert, 17
The Mischmasch (scrapbook),
27
monkeys, 72–73
Morse, Samuel, 40
Murdoch, Alice, 59–60
Murdoch, Sir Thomas, 59

N

negatives, 41
Niépce, Joseph Nicéphore, 37,
38–40
Nightingale, Florence, 45
nitrocellulose, 44–45
*No. 195: Liddell, Alice
Pleasance, facing
forward* (Dodgson),
73–74
nude images made by
Dodgson, 85

O

The Origin of Species (Darwin),
73
Ottewill & Company, 35, 42,
48
Oxford (city), 19
Oxford Movement, 22, 23
Oxford Museum of Natural
History, 72
Oxford University, 19–25.
See also Christ Church,
Oxford
Oxonian Advertiser, 27

P

Parrish, Morris Longstreth,
2–3
Parrish & Company, 2
Parrish Room, Princeton
University, 1–4
Pencil of Nature (Talbot), 42
Photographical Society of
London, 58
photography
and advertising, 43–44
and albums, 66
archives of, 55, 66, 98
beggar-girl image, 5–8,
84–86, 96, 98

Rejlander, Oscar, 64
royal family, 68
Rugby School, 15–18
Ruskin, John, 21, 31

stammer of Dodgson, 13, 16,
    23, 72
studio of Dodgson, 74, 75
summertime, 71–72

S

Salisbury, Robert Cecil,
    Marquess of, 21, 75
Schönbein (chemist), 44
sexuality of Dodgson, 16–17,
    85–86
Skeffington Lutwidge, Robert,
    35–36
skeletons, animal, 72–73
Skene, W. B., 92
smoking, Dodgson's
    abhorrence of, 56
snapshots (term), 71
"Solitude" (Dodgson), 28, 29
Southey, Reginald
    albums of, 8–9
    and camera purchase, 48
    and deanery garden, 33–34
    early results of, 55–56
    and Liddell family, 33
    and skeleton series,
        72–73
    and wet-plate collodion
        process, 43, 51

T

Tait, Archibald, 17–18
Talbot, William Fox, 41–42,
    44, 63
Tenniel, John, 89
Tennyson, Alfred
    "The Beggar Maid," 9–10,
        82
    portraits of, 73, 82, 83
Thomas, R. W., 48
Thomas Ottewill Registered
    Double Folding camera,
        48–50, 68
Train (magazine), 27, 28–29
travels of Dodgson, 66–67

U

University of Cambridge, 21
University of Oxford, 19–25.
    See also Christ Church,
    Oxford
Useful and Instructive Poetry
    (magazine), 18